T0277428

"What a welcome addition to Sheri Van Dijk's dialectical behavior thera[ ] incorporates trauma work in a gentle way, drawing on Van Dijk's knowledg[ ] how its internal parts work. Exercises facilitate and deepen learning. Throughout the book, Van Dijk encourages the reader to be patient, going at a pace comfortable for them. This book is a treasure for the layperson or clinical professional."

> —**Betsy Landau, PhD**, NYS-licensed psychologist in private practice

"Whether used as an adjunct to therapy or as a self-help guide, this workbook adeptly offers readers a plethora of practical bottom-up and top-down strategies to support healing and wellness. Through an integrative approach that expertly balances psychoeducation and skills among multiple trauma-informed modalities, the reader is provided with therapeutic tools that support reflection, personal meaning-making, and ultimately meaningful change."

> —**Jillian Hosey, MSW, RSW, LICSW**, eye movement desensitization and reprocessing (EMDR) trainer, ISSTD fellow, and coeditor of *The Handbook of Complex Trauma and Dissociation in Children*

"As a clinical trauma therapist, *The Dialectical Behavior Therapy Skills Workbook for CPTSD* is a must-read. This book offers a practical guide to understanding and healing from complex trauma. It explains how trauma affects life, and introduces DBT skills for distress tolerance, mindfulness, emotion regulation, and building connections. The workbook empowers individuals to enhance their strengths and lead fulfilling lives, making it an essential resource for individuals and clinicians."

> —**Eliza Fernandes, MSW, RSW**, founder and clinical director of a private practice specializing in trauma, with more than twenty-two years of experience in the field

"Learning behavioral skills with Sheri Van Dijk is like learning astrophysics from Neil deGrasse Tyson: a topic that could be complicated to the point of overwhelming becomes relatable, fun, and inspiring. While polyvagal theory, DBT, and ego-state therapy each offer vital resources for healing from complex trauma, it can be difficult to access them all in one place. This workbook offers a beautiful synthesis of ideas and practices from all three approaches."

> —**Alejandra Lindan**, registered psychotherapist in private practice

"Whether you are someone looking to better understand trauma or a seasoned therapist, this book offers invaluable insights and practical guidance that will provide opportunity for reflection and enrich your therapeutic toolkit. Through the lens of polyvagal theory, parts work, and DBT, the author provides clarity and compassion in navigating the intricate terrain of trauma. Each chapter is crafted with empathy and expertise. Drawing from years of clinical experience, Sheri unravels the complexities of trauma, allowing for a transformed awareness to facilitate profound healing."

—**Jodi-Lyn Knoop, MSW, RSW**, social worker and clinical director at Turning Stones Therapy

"It felt as if you could hear the book speaking to you! It is a beyond insightful read for individuals affected by trauma and helping professionals alike. The book serves as a practical guide in understanding the transformative impact of trauma, and provides clarity and directions for trauma treatment. DBT skills are well detailed in supporting healing and recovery. I can't wait to share this book with my clients."

—**Shivani Gupta, MSW, RSW, EMDRIA**, certified therapist in EMDR; and clinical director at Oakridges Therapy Centre in Ontario, Canada

"Van Dijk has gifted us an incredible workbook that embodies the principles of trauma work through its structure, tone, and guidance. This DBT skills book is the perfect companion for both therapists and clients on the journey of healing trauma. It offers essential skills and psychoeducation, making it an invaluable resource for supporting trauma survivors. A must-have for anyone committed to trauma recovery and healing."

—**Zainib Abdullah, MSW, RSW, RYT**, founder and executive director at Wellnest, a psychotherapy clinic in Toronto, Canada

The Dialectical Behavior Therapy Skills Workbook

— *for* —

CPTSD

Heal from Complex Post-Traumatic
Stress Disorder, Find Emotional Balance,
and Take Back Your Life

SHERI VAN DIJK, MSW

New Harbinger Publications, Inc.

Publisher's Note

NEW HARBINGER PUBLICATIONS is a registered trademark of New Harbinger Publications, Inc.

New Harbinger Publications is an employee-owned company.

Copyright © 2024 by Sheri Van Dijk

New Harbinger Publications, Inc.
5720 Shattuck Avenue
Oakland, CA 94609
www.newharbinger.com

Cover design by Amy Daniel

Acquired by Tesilya Hanauer

Edited by Diedre Hammons

Printed in the United States of America

26   25   24

10   9   8   7   6   5   4   3   2   1   First Printing

This book is dedicated to my clients: Your strength, persistence, and unwavering commitment to reclaiming your well-being inspire me every day. Thank you for allowing me to join you on your healing journey, and for your patience as I continue to learn and grow alongside you.

Contents

Part I

Introduction: What Is Trauma?

Complex trauma. Post-traumatic stress disorder. Developmental trauma. Attachment trauma. Emotion dysregulation. Dissociation…

If you struggle with the aftereffects of prolonged traumatic experiences, you've likely heard these and other terms before—and trust me when I say I know how confusing they can be. Or perhaps you're not familiar with these terms, which can be problematic in its own way as many of the aftereffects of trauma can be difficult to recognize, and often aren't identified by healthcare professionals, leaving people struggling to understand their experiences, thinking they're "crazy," and feeling hopeless about recovery.

Please know that there's nothing "wrong" with you; there is hope, and there is information and skills you can learn to help you get on the road to recovery. That's what this book is about.

What Is Trauma?

Psychological trauma is a response to an event that a person finds physically or emotionally threatening or harmful and overwhelms their ability to cope. Some authors have added that an experience is traumatic when one's sense of self-worth or perception of safety is damaged, one's ability to properly attribute or accept responsibility is inhibited, or one's present sense of being in control or having choices is limited (ISSTDTS 2023).

Because people experience events differently, what's traumatic for one person may not be for another; and while research suggests that approximately 90 percent of people in the United States will have at least one exposure to a traumatic event in their lifetime (Kilpatrick et al. 2013), not all will experience trauma. In a study that surveyed over 71,000 adults from twenty-six countries, the lifetime prevalence rate of post-traumatic stress disorder (PTSD) was 3.9 percent (Koenen et al. 2017) and as of 2024, according to the National Center for PTSD, about six out of every one hundred people will experience PTSD at some point in their life.

"Big T" and "Little t" Traumas

Sometimes people aren't aware their symptoms are connected to traumatic events they've experienced and this is often related to confusion about what trauma is. It can be helpful to think about two categories of trauma: "Big T" traumas are events commonly associated with the more widely recognized trauma response known as PTSD. These are typically events that most people would find highly distressing or life-threatening, such as natural disasters, serious accidents, physical or sexual assault, or war. You might also experience trauma in response to a perceived threat (where you think there's a danger, even if there actually wasn't) or threatened event. It can also be traumatic to witness something happen to someone else.

"Little t" traumas, on the other hand, are distressing events that affect individuals on a more relational level. These would be events that are not life-threatening but that still overwhelm one's ability to cope, like being bullied, finding out your partner cheated on you, or experiencing humiliation in front of your peers. Just because we refer to this as "little t" doesn't mean it's less distressing—these traumas are also very painful and can take a severe toll on physical and emotional health. Remember, what's distressing for one person may not cause the same emotional overwhelm in someone else, so the key to understanding trauma is to look at how it affects the individual rather than the event itself. Repeated exposure to "little t" traumas can cause just as much or even more emotional harm than a single "Big T" traumatic event. And, while a traumatic event might be a single event, like a car crash, it may also be chronic, such as ongoing abuse, neglect, or discrimination.

Historical trauma, when an event or prolonged experience continues to have an impact over several generations, is another way someone can experience trauma. Examples include slavery, the Holocaust, cultural and racial oppression, and forced placement in boarding schools. For example, while you're living in the twenty-first century as a free person, if your ancestors were enslaved, this traumatic experience may have been passed down to you through your family's genes, emotions, thoughts, and so on. It's also important to be aware that the harmful effects of oppression and discrimination can add layers to trauma experienced by individuals.

Post-Traumatic Stress Disorder or Complex PTSD?

PTSD and complex post-traumatic stress disorder (CPTSD) are two common diagnoses in individuals who have experienced trauma; we'll be looking in more detail at each of these diagnoses, including symptoms and diagnostic criteria, in chapter one, where you'll be able to assess which (if either) of these diagnoses makes sense for you. For now, I'll mention that the main difference is generally the frequency of the trauma: PTSD tends to be caused by a single traumatic event; CPTSD is usually related to a series of traumatic events or one prolonged event that lasts months or years. CPTSD may also include developmental trauma, when traumatic events occur early in life and disrupt normal sequences of brain development.

If you think this description of CPTSD describes you, but you haven't received a diagnosis of CPTSD, this may be because CPTSD is not recognized as a diagnosis in the *Diagnostic and Statistical Manual* (*DSM*), the publication largely used in North America to diagnose mental health problems. In 2018, CPTSD *was* included as a diagnosis in the *International Classification of Diseases* (ICD), published by the World Health Organization (WHO) and largely used throughout the rest of the world. So, whether you receive a diagnosis of CPTSD or not will depend in part on where you live and which manual is used by the professional diagnosing you.

Advocates continue to work to have CPTSD included in future editions of the *DSM* with many professionals working in the trauma field recognizing CPTSD as a separate condition that the diagnosis of PTSD doesn't fully encompass. Following are three examples to help you begin to understand "simple" PTSD, CPTSD, and CPTSD involving developmental trauma.

PTSD: Casey

Casey was working the night shift as a clerk at a convenience store when two men came in wearing masks. One of them pointed a gun at Casey and demanded she call her coworkers to the front of the store. She felt she had no choice, and when her coworkers came in, they were made to sit on the floor while the robbers ransacked the cash register and safe. It was over in minutes, but felt like it lasted for hours. They called the police and, while the men were never caught, the three coworkers were grateful no one was hurt.

For months after the robbery, Casey couldn't work. She found herself having nightmares, intrusive memories, and flashbacks, seeing the gun in her face, and hearing the threatening voices of the robbers. Even though she knew it was over and she was safe, Casey had a constant feeling of dread and the lingering belief that she was going to die. She couldn't go near the store without having a panic attack and she struggled with anxiety when she had to run errands.

CPTSD: Peter

Peter had been married to Amelia for twenty-three years; they had three children, the youngest now sixteen. Everyone thought they were a happy, successful couple, but what they didn't see was that Amelia's drinking was out of control. She was verbally and emotionally abusive to Peter when she was drinking and there were even times when she would hit him. One night, in an alcoholic rage at their son for coming home late, Amelia grabbed him by the arm and dislocated his shoulder. They lied at the hospital and said he had fallen down the stairs.

Living with Amelia's drinking and her abusive behavior for so long, Peter was constantly filled with dread. His sleep and physical health were suffering, he worried incessantly about when Amelia would go on a rampage again, and he walked on eggshells trying to prevent this from happening. Peter felt a lot of shame—for being in this situation where he felt like he had no control, for being a bad father and unable to protect his children, and for being a bad husband that Amelia had turned to drinking in the first place. He was also isolating himself, unable to bear the exhaustion of having to pretend all the time, and not wanting others to see the reality of his life.

CPTSD Involving Developmental Trauma: Marlowe

Marlowe was the oldest of four children and her parents divorced when she was ten. She and her siblings stayed with their mom, who was bitter and resentful and never let them forget that their dad had left them. Her words hurt them regularly: they were never good enough, their attempts to help around the house were always criticized, and she was very vocal about her disappointments, yelling and screaming her frustrations at them.

Now twenty-four years old, Marlowe was beginning to realize that it wasn't normal or acceptable for her mother to drag her up the stairs by her hair, or to choke her, just because Marlowe had done something she didn't like. She was also realizing how neglected she and her siblings had been as children, recalling her mother's refusal to buy her deodorant or shampoo and how she had often gone to school in clothes that were so worn you could see through the fabric.

As a young adult, Marlowe struggled with feelings of worthlessness and she had a hard time setting healthy limits in her relationships with others, often trying to please others at the cost of meeting her own needs. She was living on an emotional rollercoaster, struggling with depression at times, and regularly experiencing high anxiety.

Now that you know a bit about PTSD and CPTSD (remember, you'll learn more about these disorders and their symptoms in the next chapter), I'm going to briefly introduce the idea of a triphasic approach to treating CPTSD before we look at what else you'll learn in this book.

Stages of Treatment for Complex Trauma

Dr. Judith Herman is the psychiatrist and scholar who proposed CPTSD as a new diagnosis in her book *Trauma and Recovery* (1992). At that time, Dr. Herman also proposed that, when working with clients with complex trauma, therapists should take a staged approach to treatment. Although different authors use different names for these stages, many agree that treatment of individuals with CPTSD should follow this roadmap. Keep in mind that if you're not working with a therapist, you'll still want to follow the basics of these three stages to make the work you do as safe and effective as possible.

Stage One: Safety and Stabilization

If you're working with a therapist, this stage starts with building the therapeutic relationship so you'll feel safe for the trauma-processing work of stage two. In stage one, your therapist will help you identify the issues that brought you to therapy (with a focus on the present, rather than delving into past traumas) and will provide education about trauma and its effects. Your therapist will also teach you skills to manage emotions more effectively and to create safety and stability both internally (for instance, eliminating suicidal, self-harming, and self-destructive behaviors) and externally (such as assisting with stable housing, finances, or relationships). For clients who are highly dissociative (which we'll discuss in chapter two), stage one will also focus on stabilizing the internal system of parts (or self-system) through parts work.

If you're not working with a therapist, we'll do this work in the chapters to come. Just keep in mind that this workbook can't replace working with a therapist, and if you need help, please connect with someone for support.

Stage Two: Trauma Resolution

Stage two of complex trauma treatment usually happens with a therapist. This is the stage where processing the past traumas happens such that memories are no longer disturbing, and if necessary, trauma-based beliefs about the self are addressed.

It's important to recognize that you may not be willing or able to engage in stage two work; this will depend on your emotional, physical, and financial resources—engaging in trauma resolution therapy takes time, energy, and money. There may also be other reasons you choose not to engage in trauma processing: you may feel you're "well enough" after stage one and don't want to risk becoming destabilized by memory processing; you may have physical health problems or responsibilities such as children or work; or other considerations that lead you to forgo stage two work. For example, if you're currently undergoing medical testing for unexplained symptoms, this can be destabilizing. If that's the case, you may find that doing stage one work allows you to be sufficiently prepared to make healthy changes in stage three.

Stage Three: Integration

If you do engage in stage two work, after the resolution of trauma, you'll likely find yourself more able to move on from the past by integrating the changes within yourself and your daily life, strengthening the gains you've made, and focusing on longer-term goals to build a life worth living (Linehan 1993). This includes finding fulfillment through things like building a career, developing healthy relationships, and so on. Stage three might also involve addressing identity-related questions such as who you are now that you're no longer held back by your trauma and learning problem-solving and other skills to manage more "ordinary" problems in life.

It's important to remember that these stages of treatment aren't necessarily linear and you may find yourself shifting back and forth between stages at times.

What Stage Are You Ready For?

From the stages I've just described, you might already be aware of where you are and where you'd like to be. Answer the following questions to help you consider this.

Stage One: Safety and Stabilization

1. In the last three months, have you engaged in destabilizing behaviors, such as self-harming, suicidal behaviors, problematic substance use, disordered eating, or other self-destructive behaviors? If so, what was the behavior and when was the last time you turned to it?

    _____

    _____

    _____

    _____

2. Over the last three months, have you found yourself feeling out of control with emotions? For example, lashing out at others or having panic attacks or high anxiety.

    _____

    _____

3. Over the last three months, have you found yourself dissociating? (If you're not sure what this means, you can leave this question for now—we'll look at this in more detail in chapter two).

    _____

    _____

4. In the last three months, have you experienced external instability in your life? For example, changes in housing or finances, abuse, bullying, discrimination, or harassment?

    _____

    _____

5. In the last three months, have you found yourself struggling to meet your basic health needs, such as sleeping too much or too little, eating too much or too little, or not treating physical health problems (e.g., diabetes, thyroid, or blood pressure)?

_____

_____

6. If you responded yes to any of the above questions, you're probably in stage one and would benefit from increasing stability before deciding whether to move to stage two. Much of this book focuses on stage one, so keep reading! If you answered no to the above questions, move on to the next set of questions to determine if you'd benefit from stage two work.

Stage Two: Trauma Resolution

1. When you think of the trauma you experienced, does it feel like it's still happening on some level in the present (even if you know logically it's not)?

_____

_____

2. Do you find yourself struggling in relationships with others? For example, avoiding relationships, often putting others' needs before your own ("people-pleasing"), taking responsibility for others' emotions, or worrying that people will leave you?

_____

_____

3. When you think of the trauma, is there a sense of denial of the event or imagining that it happened to someone else?

_____

_____

4. When you think of the trauma, do you blame yourself? Or believe it means something negative about you as a person?

_____

_____

If you answered no to these questions, you may be able to do without stage two and move on to stage three work, so feel free to move on to questions about stage three, or you can consider the questions in the next section. Many of the skills in this workbook will be helpful for you in stage three, so keep reading!

If you answered yes to any of these questions, you'll likely benefit from stage two work. Keep in mind, however, that processing the trauma is typically difficult work involving intense emotions as memories are processed. Therefore, ask yourself the following questions to help determine if you're ready to do this work:

1. Consider what kind of support you'll need from others.

_____

_____

_____

2. Do you have people in your life to support you while you do this work?

_____

_____

3. Are you in good physical health?

_____

_____

4. Do you currently have the time to commit to doing this work?

_____

_____

5. Do you have the financial means to commit to the full course of therapy?

_____

_____

Even if you've decided to move into stage two and you think you're ready for it based on your answers to these questions, you can never have enough tools in your toolbox, so I'd suggest you keep reading!

Stage Three: Integration

The following questions will give you a better sense of what kind of work you'll need to focus on in stage three. If you know that you're not yet ready for this stage, I'd suggest you skip this part so you don't become overwhelmed thinking about the work to come later; some of these issues may naturally be resolved during trauma resolution.

1. Who are you now that the trauma is no longer holding you back?

_____

_____

2. What are your values and beliefs? What's important to you in life?

_____

_____

3. What are your goals for the future?

_____

_____

4. What gives you a sense of fulfillment in life?

_____

_____

5. Are you happy with your current relationships? Do you have enough people in your life and are these relationships healthy and satisfying?

_____

_____

6. Are there relationships you need to look at ending? If so, do you have the skills to end them?

_____

_____

As I mentioned earlier, many of the skills in this book will help you with stage three work as well. Now that you're starting to get a better idea of what your roadmap to recovery will look like, let's look at how this book will help.

What You'll Learn in This Book

The main focus of this book will be on stage one: learning about the effects of trauma, making sense of your symptoms, and learning skills to help you manage emotions more effectively. This will better position you to decide if you want to move on to stage two, which may or may not need to happen for you to work on stage three goals. Many of the skills you'll learn in this book can also be used in stage three. I'll refer to these stages as we go to help you figure out where you are on the roadmap. For now, let's look at what else you'll be learning in this book to help on your journey to recovery.

This book is divided into two parts. In part one, while you'll learn some skills to help you manage symptoms, the focus is on helping you understand trauma and your symptoms and increasing acceptance and hope. Chapter one will look more closely at the diagnoses of PTSD and CPTSD, the symptoms of each, and the difference between these two diagnoses.

In chapter two, you'll learn about *dissociation*, one of the common symptoms of both PTSD and, to a greater extent, CPTSD. We'll look at one of the theories that helps us understand how dissociation (as parts of the personality) can develop as a survival mechanism in people experiencing chronic childhood abuse or neglect. In chapter three, you'll learn the basics of Polyvagal Theory to help you understand more about the effects of trauma, and some of the physiological symptoms you may be experiencing, and then we'll look at strategies to help you manage these symptoms.

In part two of this book, you'll learn skills to help you manage the trauma symptoms you've been reading about. In chapters four to nine, we'll look at skills from dialectical behavior therapy (DBT), a treatment created by Dr. Marsha Linehan to help people who struggle with severe emotion dysregulation. There are four skills modules in DBT: core mindfulness, to help us live our lives more in the present and increase our ability to accept whatever we find in the present; distress tolerance, to help us manage distress and get through crisis situations without making them worse; emotion regulation, which teaches us information about emotions as well as skills to help us manage them; and interpersonal effectiveness, which helps us be more effective in developing and maintaining healthy relationships.

In chapters five and seven, we'll also look more closely at parts or self-states to help increase awareness of your internal conflicts and experiences (this is also commonly used in stage two treatment). Through learning and regularly practicing these and other skills you'll learn in this book, you'll be more able to manage your trauma symptoms.

In chapter ten, I'll discuss some of the other therapies that have been found to be most effective in processing trauma, which will be helpful if you choose to move into stage two. There are also materials available for download at the website for this book: http://www.newharbinger.com/53103.

Who This Book Is For

Because our understanding of trauma is still developing (take, for example, the fact that the DSM and the ICD can't even agree on a diagnosis of CPTSD!), the journey of individuals experiencing the consequences of trauma often remains confusing and uncertain. I decided I needed to write this book to help clients understand their experience of trauma, including how the multiple levels trauma affects us, and to incorporate different treatment models and theoretical perspectives (like Polyvagal Theory, parts work, and DBT) to address these many layers. So, if you or someone you care about has experienced trauma, or has a diagnosis of PTSD or CPTSD, and you want to learn more about what this means and what to do about it, this book will be helpful.

If you work with people who have experienced trauma, I believe this book will also speak to you by providing a lens through which to see your clients to help them make sense of their often-confusing symptoms. By increasing our understanding of the consequences of trauma on the body and mind, we can help our clients understand themselves, which often leads to an increase in self-compassion.

Much of the time, *not* having self-compassion is one of the many consequences of complex trauma, which only perpetuates individuals' suffering.

Whatever your reasons for reading this book, I thank you for joining me on this journey.

CHAPTER ONE

PTSD and Complex PTSD: Making Sense of Symptoms

If you're still reading, you're clearly dealing with some kind of trauma or helping people who are, so I'm sure I don't have to tell you how complicated trauma can be. But did you know that people often have symptoms they don't connect to events from their past? People may have had experiences they don't recognize as traumatic—usually, these are the "little t" traumas I mentioned.

In this chapter, we'll delve more deeply into the symptoms of PTSD and CPTSD to help you understand your own experiences better. We'll also look at the idea of *developmental trauma* and its connection to adverse childhood experiences (ACEs).

As you read through this information, you may find yourself struggling with intense emotions at times. When you find that happening, please be sure to take good care of yourself—put the book down if things become too distressing or uncomfortable. If you find this happening often, or in a way that's disrupting your life, you might skip ahead to chapters four, five, and six, where you'll learn skills to help you better manage the emotions arising. Remember, if you're currently in stage one of treating your complex trauma, safety and stabilization are the priority.

It's also important for you to know that suicidal thoughts or urges to hurt oneself aren't uncommon when you've experienced trauma. If you're having thoughts of suicide, please contact the National Suicide Prevention Lifeline at 988 for support. If you or a loved one are in immediate danger, please call 911. You're not alone—help is available.

PTSD Versus CPTSD

In the last chapter, I mentioned that CPTSD is not currently a diagnosis in the *DSM* but it was included in the most recent edition of the *ICD*. This illustrates the ongoing controversy regarding the diagnosis of CPTSD, with some academics believing there's not enough of a difference between the two disorders to warrant a separate category of CPTSD. Unfortunately, this often leads to people receiving diagnoses such as major depressive disorder, bipolar disorder, or an anxiety disorder that doesn't acknowledge the roots of difficulties in traumatic experiences. Whether you've received diagnoses such as these or a diagnosis of CPTSD (or perhaps you haven't received a diagnosis at all, but you recognize that you're experiencing the fallout of trauma), our discussion must start with PTSD. In the following section, you'll answer some questions to help you better understand what you're dealing with.

Symptoms of PTSD

The first requirement for a diagnosis of PTSD is that you've experienced some kind of shocking, scary, or dangerous event. Many healthcare professionals recognize the problem with this criterion since what is traumatic for one person may not be for the next. This will also depend on the developmental stage of the person experiencing the trauma. For instance, this criterion will often lead to people who have experienced attachment wounding being ineligible for a diagnosis of CPTSD; however, for a child, being left to cry alone for hours in their bedroom would possibly be experienced as a shocking or scary event. Keeping these things in mind, consider the traumatic events you've experienced. If you'd like, you can write the events here, although I'd suggest simply giving them a title (for instance, "my car accident" or "childhood abuse") rather than including details.

_____   _____

_____   _____

_____   _____

Following is a list of the three categories of PTSD symptoms according to the *ICD* (Cloitre et al. 2018). Put a check beside the symptoms you're experiencing.

Reexperiencing Symptoms

☐ Distressing dreams or nightmares of or related to the traumatic event

☐ Flashbacks (powerful memories) or intense images that come into your mind in which you feel you're reliving the experience

Avoidance

☐ Avoiding internal reminders of the experience (thoughts, feelings, and physical sensations)

☐ Avoiding external reminders of the experience (people, places, conversations, or situations)

Sense of Threat

☐ Startling easily or feeling jumpy

☐ Feeling hyper-alert, watchful, or on guard

The above symptoms are only considered symptoms of PTSD if they significantly impact your life in terms of relationships, daily activities, or work. Keep in mind, however, that you're not looking to self-diagnose but to increase your understanding of what's going on for you. Let's look now at CPTSD.

Symptoms of CPTSD

To receive a diagnosis of CPTSD, you must first meet the criteria of PTSD. The additional symptoms of CPTSD—referred to as *disturbances of self-organization*—follow. Put a check mark beside the ones you experience.

☐ Difficulties managing emotions (such as exploding in anger, feeling numb or "shutdown," having difficulties calming or soothing yourself after a stressor)

☐ Having a negative self-view (for example, believing you're worthless or "a failure;" feeling different from other people; feelings of helplessness, guilt, or shame)

☐ Having difficulties in relationships or feeling close to others (such as avoiding relationships or developing unhealthy relationships similar to those from your past)

CPTSD usually results from experiencing multiple traumatic events or prolonged exposure to trauma, and the trauma is often interpersonal in nature—that is, resulting from mistreatment by another person. Examples of common traumas in CPTSD include child abuse, neglect, or abandonment; domestic violence; bullying; torture; being a refugee separated from family and country; and discrimination.

Not everyone who experiences these kinds of events will develop PTSD or CPTSD: some people who experience a single-event trauma may develop CPTSD and some people who have experienced ongoing or recurring trauma may develop PTSD. Factors that increase the risk of CPTSD include the harm having been caused by someone close to you; being in a situation where escape or rescue was unlikely or impossible; growing up without a stable life structure (Gold 2008); and experiencing trauma at an early age, which leads to our next concepts: adverse childhood experiences and developmental trauma.

Adverse Childhood Experiences

In 1998, researchers mailed a questionnaire to 13,494 adults in the United States, inquiring about their experience of seven adverse childhood experiences (ACEs): psychological, physical, or sexual abuse; violence against mother; or living with people who used substances, had a mental illness, or were imprisoned.

Based on the responses they received, the researchers found a strong relationship between exposure to ACEs and heightened risk for seven of the ten leading causes of death in adults in the United States as well as increased risk of depression and suicide (Felitti et al. 1998). This led to the development of the Adverse Childhood Experiences Scale, often used by healthcare providers as it recognizes the toll that trauma takes on us emotionally as well as physically. You may be interested to know that this research continues and different adverse experiences have been studied in diverse populations, leading to an expanded version of the ACEs that includes experiences such as bullying, discrimination, and having lived in foster care (Pachter et al. 2017).

Let's look at how these ACEs contribute to CPTSD.

Developmental Trauma

Developmental trauma (van der Kolk 2005) refers to complex trauma that occurs during the developmental stages of childhood or adolescence. This is often referred to as *attachment trauma*, as it commonly occurs in relationships with caregivers when the child's sense of safety and trust is damaged through abuse, neglect, or unpredictable care from a primary caregiver. Examples of developmental trauma include physical or sexual assault or witnessing domestic violence. But this type of trauma also includes the "little t" traumas, such as disruptions of protective caregiving, and pervasive invalidation—when people around you continually convey that your experience doesn't matter or is somehow wrong (Linehan 2014). As noted earlier, these "little t" traumas can seem life-threatening for a child given their reliance on others for survival, especially when the events are ongoing or repetitive.

While some developmental traumas may result from intentional behavior (such as abuse), this can also be related to circumstances beyond a caregiver's control, as in the following examples:

- A child is more sensitive and has higher emotional needs than the rest of the family and the family continuously struggles to understand and support them

- A caregiver is emotionally unavailable or absent (for example, a parent works eighty-hour weeks; is hospitalized for a prolonged period or on several different occasions; or grew up in a family where it wasn't acceptable to express emotions, so they don't have the skills to deal with emotions in their own children)

- A parent relying on the child for emotional support

While developmental trauma is not an official diagnosis in the *DSM* or the *ICD*, it's important for us to be aware of it for a number of reasons: Since traumatic events occur during the time of life when the brain is still developing, healthy, normative development might not occur and the brain instead adapts to the trauma it faces. For example, studies have shown that the amygdala (the alarm center of the brain) is larger in youth who have grown up in hostile environments (Picci et al. 2022); levels of stress hormones are also higher (Bevans et al. 2008). These differences can be seen as helping the youth survive the difficult circumstances faced at the time, but they can contribute to ongoing problems that may result in inaccurate diagnoses, such as ADHD, bipolar disorder, and oppositional defiant disorder, leading to inappropriate treatments (which can include medications that may be unnecessary for some individuals) rather than therapy to address the trauma they've experienced (van der Kolk 2005). Developmental trauma can also result in a child growing up with low self-esteem and self-worth, feelings of shame, and ongoing difficulties with relationships and emotion regulation as well as other symptoms of CPTSD.

One more thing that will be helpful for you to know: even if traumatic events happened at such a young age that you can't recall them, they can still have long-term negative consequences (such as symptoms of PTSD and CPTSD) since developmental trauma affects the development of the brain. This is how, as Dr. Bessel van der Kolk (2014) says, "the body keeps the score": our body remembers even when we don't have the words to go along with the memory. When we're having an implicit memory (a memory for which we don't have explicit, cognitive recall), we experience emotions, physical sensations, and urges without recognizing the influence of the past on our present. This is what people sometimes refer to as an "emotional flashback."

So, when you don't understand why you have a panic attack when someone tries to hug you, for example, it's possible that this is your body remembering a trauma (it could also be related to your fear of germs, of course, but if you have trauma in your past, it's important to consider!). We'll explore some of these physiological responses in chapter three and you'll learn some ways to work with them.

Now that you have a better idea of what these different terms mean and how they may apply to you, let's consider why some people develop PTSD, others develop CPTSD, and others don't experience a trauma response at all in the face of the same events.

Activity: Risk Factors for Trauma

In the following activity, you'll consider some of the different factors that increase your likelihood of developing a trauma response. If you've experienced more than one traumatic event, you can answer the questions for those events generally, you can write your answers on a separate worksheet for each trauma you've experienced (I would recommend against this if you've had more than two single-event traumas), or you can come up with a way that feels most comfortable for you. Remember to be aware of yourself as you go through this exercise and put it aside if you need to. You can always return to it later.

1. **Family History**

   If you have a family history of mental health problems, your risk of developing PTSD or CPTSD is increased. What do you know about your family history?

   _____

   _____

   _____

   _____

2. **Ongoing Stress**

   Experiencing ongoing stress at the time of a traumatic event contributes to your risk of developing a trauma response. Consider any destabilizing events or ongoing stressors at the time of the events (such as financial or housing instability, the break-up of a relationship, or being a primary caregiver for a child with special needs or an elderly parent).

   _____

   _____

   _____

   _____

3. **Poor Coping Skills**

   People who don't have healthy coping skills are generally at higher risk for developing a trauma response. Do you have healthy ways of managing distress (like exercising, talking to friends, or distracting yourself in healthy ways)? Or do you turn to unhealthy ways of coping (like using food, substances, or other problematic behaviors to avoid emotions)? Write your thoughts about how you were coping at the time of the events here:

   _____

   _____

   _____

   _____

4. **History of Substance Use**

   People with a history of substance use also have a heightened risk for PTSD or CPTSD. Did this apply to you when you experienced the events?

   _____

   _____

   _____

   _____

5. **The Supports You Have After the Events**

   Research has consistently shown that having a warm and supportive social network (including family, friends, and helping professionals) makes a trauma response less likely. What do you recall about your support system after the events?

   _____

   _____

   _____

   _____

6. **Interpretations and Perceptions of the Events**

    The way we think about an event also contributes to our vulnerability to developing a trauma response. What were your thoughts and beliefs about what happened? Include any judgmental or blaming thoughts (toward yourself or others), as well as any meaning you made of the events (such as thinking "This happened to me because I deserved it" or "Sometimes, bad things happen to good people").

    _____

    _____

    _____

    _____

7. **History of Developmental Trauma**

    Developmental trauma affects the healthy development of the brain, which can leave you more vulnerable to emotion dysregulation and contribute to difficulties with assertiveness, setting healthy limits, and so on. Write your thoughts about how this might apply to you here:

    _____

    _____

    _____

    _____

Take a moment to consider your responses to these questions. What are your thoughts about your risk factors for developing a trauma response? Describe any thoughts and emotions that have come up for you:

_____

_____

_____

_____

I mentioned earlier that I'm not trying to help you self-diagnose but to understand your experience better. I'll also point out that many survivors of trauma don't meet the criteria for PTSD and they may still be experiencing consequences of the trauma, such as difficulties managing emotions, substance use issues, eating disorders, and chronic physical health problems. If you're finding yourself fitting into this category as you're reading through these various symptoms, please know that you can still benefit from the information and skills you'll be learning in this book, so keep reading!

If you are resonating with what you're reading here, then you're obviously on the right track. In the next chapter, you'll learn about dissociation and how it's possible for human beings to so effectively protect themselves from a trauma that they actually forget it ever happened (at one extreme), or to compartmentalize it so they can go about their normal life in spite of it. Even if you don't think this applies to you, I'd encourage you to keep reading since we don't know what we don't know. I often work with clients with a trauma history who don't have a full understanding of their symptoms. I've also learned the hard way in my work that dissociative symptoms are often overlooked by mental health professionals, so you may find you're more able to make sense of your experience through this lens. Please remember to keep taking good care of yourself as you go: this is hard work and our number one goal is getting you stable and keeping you there.

Wrapping Up

In this chapter, you've been learning about trauma—what it is and the difference between PTSD and CPTSD—and you've learned to identify some of the symptoms associated with these diagnoses. You've also had the opportunity to learn about developmental trauma and to consider some of the factors that may have heightened your risk for developing a trauma response. One of the most important pieces in stage one of trauma treatment is learning about trauma and its negative consequences; while this can be uncomfortable, I hope that over time you'll find it validating to know that this is an ordinary response to the extraordinary events you've experienced—and that you're not alone with these symptoms.

In the next chapter, you'll continue to learn about symptoms of trauma, with a specific focus on dissociation—experiences that are complex and can be frightening. If at any time what you're reading starts to evoke emotions that are too distressing, please be sure to do some self-care; you can also turn to chapter four, which will teach you some skills to help you better manage distress.

CHAPTER TWO

Understanding Dissociation

You may already be familiar with the term dissociation, and you may have a good understanding of how this shows up in your life (or doesn't!). But just as we've been learning more and more about trauma over recent decades, so too do we continue to learn more about dissociation, including how to define it and understand how and why it happens. Controversy remains about certain dissociative experiences as does a lack of understanding and awareness of these processes.

My goal in this chapter, therefore, is to help you understand what dissociation is, that it can happen in different ways, and that the term "dissociation" itself refers to a broad range of experiences. Then we'll look at ways you might be experiencing this phenomenon. In the second part of this chapter, you'll learn more about how and why dissociation may have developed for you, and in the second part of this book, we'll get to skills to help you increase awareness of these experiences so you'll be more able to do something about them. First, let's arm you with information.

What Is Dissociation?

The answer to this question is complicated as there is still not one agreed-upon definition, so we'll start here: According to the International Society for the Study of Trauma and Dissociation (ISSTD), dissociation involves "the total or partial loss of awareness or knowledge, inner body sensation, five-sense perception (sight, hearing taste, touch, and smell), emotions, thoughts, perceptions, explicitly recallable memories, impulses, and/or one's sense of self" (ISSTDTS 2023, 27). In other words, there are lots of ways dissociation can occur, but it involves a disconnect between you and your present experience.

Dissociation occurs on a spectrum: there is "normal" dissociation that everyone has at times—when you're driving and you suddenly realize you don't remember part of the drive or you're so absorbed in reading a book that you're unaware of what's happening around you. These are examples of non-pathological dissociation.

But what if you sometimes feel like you're disconnected from the world around you or like you're a robot someone else is controlling? Or you're going about your day and you suddenly realize an hour has gone by and you have no idea what happened during that time? These are some of the problematic (not to mention scary!) ways dissociation can happen. While dissociation is, of course, a symptom of dissociative disorders (such as dissociative identity disorder, or DID), dissociation can also be a symptom of PTSD and CPTSD and commonly occurs in people with other diagnoses as well, like depression, anxiety, and borderline personality disorder (BPD). Dissociation can be frightening, especially if you're convinced that it means something about you as a person (like, *I'm crazy*); understanding your experience can help you be less fearful of it.

Activity: Experiencing Dissociation

Following is a brief description of the five main dissociative processes, followed by some statements. Consider each statement carefully: if you've never experienced it or if you don't understand the statement (it likely doesn't apply to you), leave it blank. If you've ever experienced it, put a check beside it.

Depersonalization

This is the sense of being disconnected from or "not in" your body, or feeling detached from yourself in some way ("This is not me"). This might entail experiences that are hard for you to put into words; for example, one client I worked with kept telling me she felt "anxious," but she didn't report feeling worried or afraid. When she told me she felt "as though someone else is in my body," we realized this was depersonalization.

☐ I've felt as though I'm standing next to myself or watching myself do something as if I was looking at another person.

☐ I've looked in the mirror and not recognized myself.

☐ Parts of my body have felt as though they didn't belong to me.

☐ My body has felt very light, as if it were floating on air.

☐ When I've cried or laughed, I seemed to not feel any emotions at all.

☐ When I moved, it seemed as though I was not in charge of my movements, so I felt like a robot.

Derealization

In derealization, the world seems unreal or dreamlike, foggy, or distant. One of my clients described her experience of this as feeling "like I'm in a video game."

☐ I've felt like other people, objects, or the world in general were not real.

☐ I've felt as though I was looking at the world through a fog, with people or objects appearing far away or unclear.

☐ It's seemed as if things I've recently done took place a long time ago (for example, something I did earlier in the day felt like I had done it weeks ago).

☐ Objects around me have looked smaller or farther away.

☐ Previously familiar places or people have looked unfamiliar, as if I'd never seen them before.

Amnesia

Different from routine forgetfulness, dissociative amnesia is when you have no memory of something, either in the recent or distant past. This might show up as having no memory before a certain age. For example, one of my clients was abused by her brother from age twelve to eighteen. She had told me her brother was coming to visit, but when I asked about this in our next session, she couldn't remember if the visit had happened.

☐ I've found myself in a place with no idea of how I got there.

☐ I've found evidence that I've done things I have no memory of (like errands or sending an email to someone).

☐ Others have told me of things that I had done, but I had no memory of doing those things.

☐ I've "lost time," with no memory of what happened during that period (blank spells or blackouts).

☐ There have been times when I haven't recognized family members or close friends.

Identity Confusion

This is when you feel as though your identity has shifted and you don't have a good sense of who you are, what your values are, what you like and dislike, and so on. For example, one of my clients would have thoughts of acting violently toward people, but the thoughts were disturbing for him because they didn't match his values and who he wanted to be.

- ☐ I've felt confused or puzzled by the way I feel, or by things I've said or done.

- ☐ I've felt divided, like I had several independent "parts" or aspects of myself.

- ☐ I've often felt like I'm "different" from myself.

- ☐ At times, my thoughts and emotions have been so changeable I didn't understand myself.

- ☐ I've experienced a struggle inside myself regarding what to think, feel, or do.

Identity Alteration

At its extreme, this is where a person has DID and shifts to a different part (or self-state) that may not know where they are, how old they are, and so on. But this can also happen in less extreme ways: like feeling as though there's a different part of you acting at times, and that part doesn't feel like the *real* you. For example, one of my clients will suddenly feel herself shutting down and can explain that she feels "childlike," but she doesn't have awareness of what she's feeling or why.

- ☐ I've felt like I have "someone else" inside or like I'm more than one person.

- ☐ I've heard voices inside my head, telling me what to do or commenting on things I'm doing.

- ☐ I've felt like someone or something else takes over at times, and I have no control over myself.

- ☐ I've been confused about how old I am or where I am.

- ☐ I've noticed different parts of myself reacting to these questions.

Take a moment to consider what it was like to read about these dissociative phenomena: Was there a sense of relief as you learned that some of your symptoms can be explained by dissociation? Or perhaps fear, shame, or other painful emotions if you related to some of these symptoms? You might have noticed conflicting thoughts and emotions and felt like there was more than one part of you responding to the questions—perhaps one part of you wanting to deny the dissociative experience and another part wanting to acknowledge it. Perhaps you didn't relate to any of these symptoms, or you're already familiar with these experiences of dissociation within yourself. Whatever you notice, do some self-care if needed; and then make some notes here:

_____

_____

_____

_____

Now that you're starting to understand what dissociation is, let's look at its purpose and how it can help us.

Dissociation in Response to Trauma

Dissociation is an adaptive mechanism that helps us survive. It develops as a defense against a perceived threat, resulting in overwhelming experiences being split off from and held outside of our conscious awareness. This is why, as Dr. Bessel van der Kolk says, "Dissociation is the essence of trauma" (2014, 66). What better way for our brain to protect us from a traumatic experience than for it to cut us off from the experience altogether? This is also why dissociation can take many forms—because trauma does, too. Let's look at an example.

Marguerite's Story

Marguerite started therapy at the age of twenty-five when she took a leave from her post-graduate studies because she was struggling to function. Her sleep was suffering because she was having panic attacks and nightmares at night; during the day, she was reliving things that had happened in her childhood.

At the age of five, Marguerite's older brother started sexually and physically abusing her. She recalled feeling "floaty" during the abuse, being outside of her body and unable to feel what was happening (depersonalization). Marguerite told her parents about the abuse, but they told her to "stop lying." So, not only did she have to deal with the abuse from her brother but she also had to suffer through her parents' denial and neglect. At times, Marguerite would look at her family and feel like she was surrounded by strangers, or she'd be sitting in her bedroom and experience her surroundings as strange and unfamiliar (derealization).

Marguerite recalled she always looked forward to going to school because that was one place she felt safe. She described being miserable at breakfast time, having to sit across the table from her brother, who had abused her the night before, but then she'd get on the bus and forget what had happened at home (amnesia). The abuse went on until Marguerite left home for college at the age of eighteen, and it was only then she began remembering what had happened to her all those years.

Speaking with her therapist about the years of abuse, Marguerite recounted her struggle to understand herself. For instance, she felt conflicted about having a relationship with her parents (identity confusion): One part of her believed her family should always come first, but another part of her hated her brother for the pain he had caused and her parents for not protecting her, resulting in internal conflict. She'd find herself on the phone with her mother, agreeing to visit even though she didn't want to and feeling like she wasn't in control of herself (identity alteration).

Activity: How Did Dissociation Help You?

Following is a list of the dissociative processes we looked at earlier. For each of the processes you experience, write your thoughts about how this helped you survive the traumatic experiences or how you might otherwise make sense of the symptom. I've used Marguerite as an example. Remember to take your time and put this aside if emotions get too intense. If you don't experience any of these symptoms, feel free to move on to the next section.

Depersonalization

How has not being in your body helped you survive? (Marguerite escaped emotional and physical pain by not being in her body.)

_____

_____

_____

_____

Derealization

How has disconnecting from the world around you helped you survive? (Marguerite was able to not feel the pain of her parents' invalidation and betrayal.)

_____

_____

_____

_____

Amnesia

How has not remembering helped you survive? (Amnesia helped Marguerite go about her daily life while she continued to live with her abusers.)

_____

_____

_____

_____

Identity Confusion

How has acting in inconsistent ways helped you survive? (As a child, Marguerite had to stay connected to her parents since she relied on them for survival—this meant staying quiet about the abuse to not risk punishment or rejection.)

_____

_____

_____

_____

Identity Alteration

How has having other parts of your personality helped you survive? (Marguerite had to do or say things to stay connected to her parents, like keeping up the pretense of being a "happy family," even when she didn't believe or like what she was saying or doing.)

_____

_____

_____

_____

If you identified some of these processes happening within you at times, what was this like? Make some notes here about anything that came up for you:

_____

_____

_____

_____

Remember, we'll look at skills to help with these experiences in the second part of this book, but increasing your awareness of these experiences is the first step in healing and recovery. Now, let's look at a theory to help us make further sense of an extreme dissociative phenomenon: when the personality itself is dissociated or fragmented.

Theory of Structural Dissociation of the Personality

There are different models that explain how dissociation develops in response to trauma, and there's likely more than one path that leads to this phenomenon. I'm going to focus on the Theory of Structural Dissociation of the Personality, or SDP (van der Hart et al. 2006), because it does a nice job of explaining how dissociation of the personality is a survival response to trauma and extreme stress in childhood, which, as you know, is common in CPTSD. If this doesn't apply to you, don't worry—in the next chapter, we'll look at another theory that also explains this.

The reality is that most people have experienced some degree of psychological wounding, so we all have parts of our personality; we might also refer to parts as *self-states*, *aspects of ourselves*, or *ego states*. Essentially, these terms refer to how we think, feel, and act changes across time and contexts. We can see this in the language we use at times: "One part of me wants to do this, but another part of me wants to do that." We also saw this in the earlier story of Marguerite, who would value or believe one thing, but then not act in accordance with that value or belief. Here are some other examples:

- Feeling angry with your partner while also being confused by why you're feeling this way ("They didn't do anything wrong, why am I so mad?")

- Sharing information you'd prefer to keep to yourself, but feeling unable to stop

- Acting in a way you know you'll regret later—for example, using substances, engaging in self-harm, or gossiping

Can you think of times when you've been aware of different parts of yourself? Make some notes here:

_____

_____

_____

_____

_____

We'll be looking further at parts of the personality, as well as how we can heal from trauma using this perspective, at different points in this book. For now, while most of us can probably relate to having parts to some extent, it's important to understand that with structural dissociation, we're moving beyond these self-states: there's a lack of integration in the personality and the self is split into parts that have their own perspectives, emotions, and thoughts. A person's early life experiences (think ACEs) and development (including genes) are two factors that play roles in structural dissociation. If you had a relatively safe, secure, and consistent childhood, your personality will have been more likely to fully develop and you'll be more likely to have a sense of self that feels integrated and whole.

To clarify, we're not talking specifically about DID. Often, when it comes to parts of the personality, people think of that extreme, but people with CPTSD, PTSD, and other disorders can also experience structural dissociation. It's also important to remember that dissociative parts of the personality are not actually separate personalities but rather are different parts or aspects of personality that are not (yet) working together cooperatively (Fisher 2017).

SDP is referred to as *structural* dissociation because the creators of this theory propose that psychological dissociation happens along the fault lines of different brain structures that would, as a course of normal development, communicate with one another (An in-depth description of this is beyond the scope of this book, so check out the Further Reading section if you want to know more). When developmental trauma results in structural dissociation, these parts of the brain split off from one another as a means of survival, allowing for more flexible responses to a dangerous environment. Although this is a survival mechanism, it results in the personality fragmenting, where one part (the normal life part) keeps on going as though nothing has occurred and other parts (trauma parts) remain alert for the next bad thing to happen.

The Normal Life Part

The *normal life part* (Fisher 2017) focuses on living life in the present, avoiding reminders of the trauma in order to focus on taking care of physical needs like sleeping and eating, going to work or school, attachment, social interaction, and other aspects of daily life. This part usually has little or no awareness of the trauma and is focused on what needs to be done today. Think again of Marguerite—she was experiencing daily abuse at home, yet her normal life part was still getting up and eating breakfast with the family, going to school, and doing other things like swimming lessons and sleepovers.

Trauma Parts

The *trauma part* of the personality (Fisher 2017) holds information related to the trauma (body memories, emotions, thoughts, beliefs, and so on), so this part is fearful that the trauma will happen again and remains on the lookout for danger. Trauma parts will be triggered by implicit or explicit reminders of the trauma and are often characterized by intense painful emotions. We can see a trauma part (or perhaps more than one) in Marguerite's reports of having nightmares, panic attacks, and flashbacks.

Primary structural dissociation is generally experienced in PTSD and involves a single normal life part and a single trauma part. *Secondary* structural dissociation involves a single normal life part and multiple trauma parts and is more likely to be seen in CPTSD or BPD. In *tertiary* structural dissociation, there are multiple normal life parts and multiple trauma parts (this is DID). The last piece we'll look at here is what trauma parts are from an SDP perspective.

Trauma Parts as Defenses

Developing early in life, defense responses help us survive. You're probably familiar with three of these already: *fight, flight,* and *freeze.* But we also have two others: *submit* and *attach* (or *cry for help*). According to SDP, these defense systems are another fault line around which trauma parts form—when a defense response such as "fight" is activated by a trauma that overwhelms our ability to cope, a self-state may form based on that defense response. So, in this example, we would end up with a "fight part."

Following is a description of trauma parts from an SDP perspective. As you read about each of these and the examples provided, consider your own experience and make some notes about any parts that seem familiar to you. Remember to prioritize self-care and take a break if things become too difficult, but it may also help to keep in mind as you read this information that, if you relate to some (or all!) of these, your parts helped you survive and are trying to protect you, even now.

The Fight Part

A fight part is usually on the lookout for threat, meaning this part will typically be mistrustful of others and ready to keep people at arm's length to protect you. Fight parts may be angry, controlling, judgmental, and blaming, and will often have a hand in self-harming, suicidal, and other self-destructive behaviors, as well as aggression toward others.

Example: *Cory recalls first thinking of suicide when he was twelve years old. He had a very controlling father who didn't understand Cory's depression and pushed Cory to do better in school, play more sports, take on more responsibilities, and so on, until Cory finally found escape through* *fantasizing about taking his life. Now, Cory is thirty years old and finds himself thinking about suicide when he feels like he has no control, even though he knows he's an adult and has choices he didn't have as a child.*

What do you know about your fight part?

_____

_____

_____

_____

The Flight Part

A flight part is looking to escape. This might be seen through a person being avoidant, distant, ambivalent, or unable to make commitments. Flight parts often turn to addictions, disordered eating, and other behaviors that provide escape from painful emotions, thoughts, and sensations.

Example: *Karmen recently left her marriage to an abusive and controlling partner. She had been using drugs for a long time to manage her emotional pain, but having finally gotten clean from these, she now finds herself alternating between restricting food and bingeing. She doesn't want to do these things but feels like she has no control over herself.*

What do you know about your Flight Part?

_____

_____

_____

_____

The Freeze Part

A freeze part is fearful, will often isolate themselves or feel paralyzed, and at the extreme may fear leaving the home. High levels of anxiety and panic attacks are common, as well as nightmares and flashbacks.

Example: *Jhavid reports constant feelings of anxiety and daily panic attacks. Bullied in school for being the only person of color and growing up with three older brothers who teased him relentlessly for being more sensitive, Jhavid still feels like nowhere is safe.*

What do you know about your freeze part?

_____

_____

_____

_____

The Submit Part

This part is the opposite of the fight part and will often present as passive, people-pleasing, and self-sacrificing, trying to be "good." Inside, however, this part often experiences shame, hopelessness, self-hatred, and depression.

Example: *Marval recalled that her mother was always yelling at her when she was a child, and even at age fifty-five, she always feels like she's doing something wrong. She goes out of her way to please others and make them like her, even when that means regularly putting aside her own needs and wants. She also has a habit of over-apologizing, constantly feeling ashamed and not good enough.*

What do you know about your submit part?

_____

_____

_____

_____

The Attach Part

An attach part feels lonely and yearns for connection to others. This part is often childlike, wants to be liked by others, wants to have others to care for them, and fears abandonment.

Example: *Sam was seeing their new therapist, Shayne, once a week and felt very connected to him, but Sam found they had a strong need to reach out to Shayne between sessions. Sam was reaching out multiple times a day by email or text and when Shayne told Sam he would only respond to them once a day moving forward, Sam felt very hurt and alone.*

What do you know about your attach part?

_____

_____

_____

_____

Normal life parts and trauma parts often interact in conflicting ways, which can lead to difficulties with emotion regulation and relationships with self and others. For instance, if you find yourself struggling to read this section—zoning out, being easily distracted, or judging what you're reading—this may be an indicator that one or more of your parts is being activated by the idea of acknowledging that you have different parts! Confusing, I know, but there is good reason for this: Remember, parts were created to protect you, and they may believe you still need protecting. In this case, thinking that the less you know about your own internal system, the better. If this still isn't making sense, don't worry—we'll be doing some work with your parts in chapter seven when we look at coming to terms with trauma.

Wrapping Up

If you're relating to what you've read in this section, remember this is just the start of your journey, and that knowledge is power. Hopefully, any confusion, shame, fear, or other emotions related to experiences of dissociation and parts will start to reduce as you start to understand them and see that these processes are adaptive and helped you to survive the traumas.

Of course, now that you're an adult, these defense mechanisms are likely no longer serving you and may even be limiting your ability to live life as you would like (for instance, at times, you may feel "spaced out," disconnected, detached). In the next chapter, you'll learn about *Polyvagal Theory*, which will help you make sense of some of the other symptoms you may be experiencing and then we'll move into strategies to help you regulate your nervous system and regain control of your life.

CHAPTER THREE

Regulating Your Nervous System

Hopefully, you're starting to understand that the trauma-related symptoms you're experiencing are normal, adaptive responses to events that overwhelmed your ability to cope at the time of the trauma and that these responses are involuntary and unconscious. In other words, you are not to blame for the way your body and mind have chosen to help you survive and through learning about these processes, you'll be more able to change the way your body and mind respond in the future.

Before we turn our focus to skills to help you manage these responses and emotions more effectively, there's one more idea that will be helpful for you to learn: Polyvagal Theory. If you didn't relate to the SDP model from the last chapter, this theory will help you make sense of your trauma-related experiences by increasing your understanding of the nervous system and the role it plays when we face extreme stress and trauma. If you did relate to the SDP model, this chapter will also further your understanding of how parts develop.

What Is Polyvagal Theory?

In 1994, Dr. Steven Porges introduced *Polyvagal Theory* to the world. This theory has become popular in helping us understand the role of our nervous system in emotion regulation, social connection, and the fear response. I'll start by defining some terms you'll need to know for our discussion of trauma; remember to check out the Further Reading section at the end of this workbook if you're interested in learning more.

Unconscious Perception: Neuroception

Neuroception is the term coined by Dr. Porges to refer to the unconscious process of our nervous system constantly (six times per second!) scanning for threats. This involves assessment of internal (such as thoughts, emotions, and physical sensations) and external (what's happening in our environment) cues, as well as what's happening between us and the people around us.

Here's an example: One night, I was driving on a quiet back road when suddenly I *felt* that I needed to brake. I slowed down, and a moment later, a deer jumped into the road in front of me, missing me by milliseconds. No, I'm not psychic!—clearly, I had unconsciously perceived something that put me on alert for danger, causing me to slow the car. This is neuroception. You might recall a situation when something similar has happened to you: perhaps a "first impression" of someone that was later confirmed ("Thank goodness I didn't go out with them for that drink!") or a job you turned down because it "didn't feel right." Of course, sometimes we get it wrong—maybe you realize later that job would've been a perfect fit for you!

If our system neurocepts cues of safety, we'll feel calm and be more able to engage with others. If we're picking up cues of danger, on the other hand, our system will prepare us for defensive action. From this perspective, we could say that anxiety is the result of an overly sensitive system that neurocepts things as threatening when they're really not.

Let's look more closely at the autonomic nervous system and how what we neurocept leads to automatic responses in our body.

The Autonomic Nervous System

The *autonomic nervous system* (ANS) involves various organs from our brain to our colon, with the vagus nerve linking them all together. When the ANS neurocepts a threat, it activates one of the defense responses you learned about in the last chapter: fight, flight, freeze, submit, or cry for help. Our ANS acts *outside of our conscious awareness*—we don't get to choose which defense mechanism is activated. This is important to be aware of as people often beat themselves up for how they responded in a traumatic or stressful situation. But I'm getting a little ahead of myself. Let's first get to know our ANS a little better from a polyvagal perspective.

Three Pathways of the Autonomic Nervous System

There are two branches of the ANS: the sympathetic nervous system (SNS), which is also referred to as the "fight-or-flight" system, and the parasympathetic nervous system (PNS), also known as the "rest and digest" system. According to Polyvagal Theory, the PNS is split into two pathways that travel within the vagus nerve: the dorsal vagal and ventral vagal—hence the name, Polyvagal Theory. The following Polyvagal Theory Chart of Trauma Response (Walker 2018) can help you understand these three zones, what each response entails physiologically, and how they help us survive (you can also see this chart in full color here: http://www.newharbinger.com/53103). This chart also illustrates how we move up the polyvagal ladder (Dana 2023) as we become more emotionally aroused and how we move back down the ladder as our system detects that we are safe and arousal decreases. In the color chart provided online, you'll see that ventral vagal is represented in green; sympathetic arousal is yellow; and dorsal vagal is red. Just like the colors of a stoplight, green means go—all clear, it's safe to proceed; yellow means caution—be on the lookout for danger; and red means STOP, there's danger (in PVT terms, life threat).

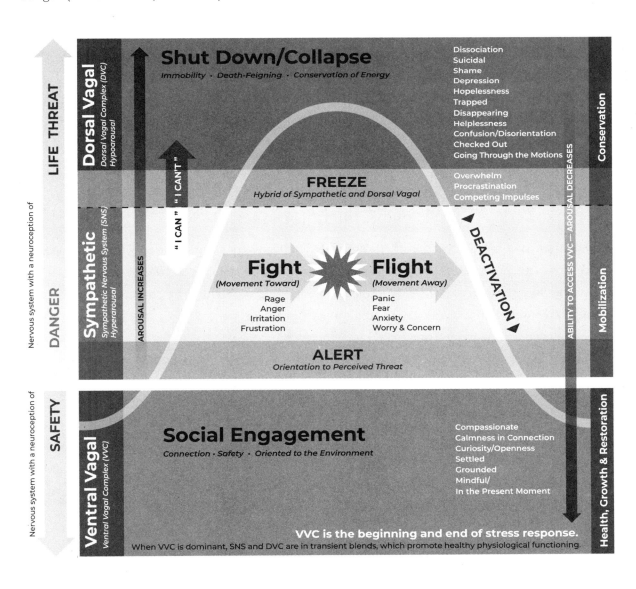

When the ventral vagal PNS pathway is activated, we feel safe, calm, and connected and we're able to engage with others. If our ANS interprets cues in our environment as threatening, our SNS kicks in, mobilizing us to act—by fighting, fleeing, or freezing. Once we've acted and our ANS neurocepts us as safe once again, we return to that ventral vagal state. But if we're in SNS arousal (fight, flight, or freeze mode) and our ANS detects that we're trapped and unable to escape, our dorsal vagal pathway will become activated, causing us to shut down to survive. In this state, we submit or collapse (which is why this is also known as "flop and drop") as our system tries to protect us from, or prepare us for, death (think of a wildebeest that's been brought down by a lion).

In the following section, we'll look at each of these states one by one before we look at an example and then have you consider what each of these looks like for you.

Ventral Vagal: Safe and Socially Engaged

When we're in this state, our heart rate is regulated and we can take in the faces of friends and family and focus on conversations without being overly distracted by noise around us. We're able to be curious, open, and interested and to feel connected to our experience and the people around us. For simplicity, I'm going to use Dana's (2018) language and call this the *green zone*—we experience ourselves as safe.

Sympathetic Arousal: Fight, Flight, or Freeze

When our system neurocepts a threat, our SNS activates, preparing our body to fight, flee, or freeze: our heart rate increases; we feel the rush of adrenaline as agitation or heat in the body; we feel anxious, nervous, or angry; and the world feels threatening, frightening, or chaotic. If we're in our SNS regularly, we might experience ongoing anxiety and even panic attacks, anger, irritability; difficulties following through on things; and problems in relationships.

This is the *yellow zone*: when we need to use caution to protect ourselves from threat.

Dorsal Vagal Shutdown: Flop and Drop

If our SNS has been activated (we're in yellow) and our ANS continues to sense a threat we're unable to escape, our dorsal vagus becomes activated. This is the system of last resort: when all else fails, our system tries to help us survive by collapsing or feigning death. Think of a possum playing dead; this is different from a sympathetic freeze, which involves energy—similar to a deer frozen in headlights, with tension in the muscles. In this shutdown state, opioids are released to numb us to any pain that might accompany the threat we're facing, and as a result, this is where we may become dissociated from our experience. When our system frequently goes into this collapsed mode, problems of daily living can include depression, dissociation, fatigue, and difficulties with memory.

This is the *red zone*: when there is life threat.

I'll just mention that there is some overlap of these states at times: for example, I enjoy stand-up paddleboarding. When I'm out on the lake, I'm happy, at peace, and feeling calm and connected to the universe (green zone), but there's also some stress in my system. My muscles are tense to help me stay balanced on the board, my heart rate and blood pressure are slightly elevated as I stay alert for dangerous boaters, and I'm working to paddle (yellow zone). We can therefore think of this as being in a blended state, or at the edges of these two systems. For simplicity, however, I'll stick to a more black-and-white conceptualization of these states.

A healthy ANS responds relatively accurately to cues of safety and danger, rather than regularly neurocepting cues as dangerous when they're not, and can move flexibly between these states, rather than remaining stuck.

What This Means If You Have Trauma

Let's put this into context by returning to Marguerite and our discussion of parts from the last chapter. Marguerite comes home from school; her brother has soccer after school, so she feels safe. She's in her bedroom doing homework, feeling calm after a good day at school with her friends—she's in her green zone. Suddenly, Marguerite hears the front door close. Her ANS automatically (and unconsciously!) moves her into yellow so she's ready to act if needed. She calls out, asking who's there, and when she hears her grandmother call up to her, she breathes a sigh of relief—Grandma is supportive and loving—and Marguerite moves back down into her green zone, anticipating warmth and affection from her.

Here's another version of this story: Marguerite comes home from school, is in her green zone as she does homework, and her system moves into yellow when she hears the door close. She calls out and when she gets no response, she knows it's her brother and they're home alone together. Marguerite moves further up the ladder in the yellow zone: she leaps up and locks her bedroom door (trying to flee). Unfortunately, that won't keep him out long and Marguerite frantically looks around, assessing her options. As she hears her brother working the lock, Marguerite's system moves into her red, shutting her down as her ANS neurocepts that there's no escape. By the time her brother gets into the room, she's already dissociating (which we can also see as Marguerite's submit part taking over to protect her).

When you've experienced trauma—prolonged and repetitive, or single-event—your system can become overly sensitive, neurocepting cues as dangerous when they're not (remember, "sense of threat" is one of the clusters of symptoms of PTSD). So, fifteen years later, Marguerite's system doesn't respond accurately to cues and continues to move her into the yellow zone—she has anxiety, panic attacks, and flashbacks—and into the red zone—causing dissociation, depression, chronic fatigue, and problems with memory even though she's no longer living in that abusive environment. Marguerite's system has been trained to be overly sensitive (a.k.a.: her parts become activated) to help her survive.

The following exercise will have you consider what each of these states looks like for you and how you can start helping your system move more fluidly from red to yellow to green.

Activity: Getting to Know Your Zones

The first step in helping your system become more flexible (for instance, being able to come back to the green zone if you know you're not actually in danger but find yourself stuck in yellow or red) is to become aware of what zone you're in. To help with this, in the following activity (based on Dana 2023), you'll make some notes describing yourself when you're in each zone. I've given you some words commonly used to describe these states to help.

How you feel in green (e.g., safe, calm, at peace, connected, engaged, mindful, curious, open, compassionate, grounded):

_____

How you feel in yellow (e.g., unsafe, on guard, worried, afraid, panicky, frustrated, irritated, angry, agitated, restless):

_____

How you feel in red (e.g., threatened, helpless, hopeless, depressed, ashamed, numb, disconnected, detached, trapped):

_____

Now that you have a better understanding of what these states feel like for you, let's look at how you behave in each state. Again, I've started you off with some examples.

What you do in green (e.g., connecting with others, focusing, laughing, playing, taking care of self, being productive):

_____

_____

_____

_____

What you do in yellow (e.g., checking, having difficulties sitting still, arguing or fighting, acting aggressively, impulsively, or recklessly):

_____

_____

_____

_____

What you do in red (e.g., dissociating, numbing, avoiding, escaping, sleeping, using substances, shutting down, engaging in self-harming or suicidal behaviors):

_____

_____

_____

_____

Next, let's look at your triggers for each of these states. What typically causes you to be in your green, yellow, and red zones? Here, I've given you some examples from Marguerite's story.

Times when you're in green (e.g., spending time with friends or my dog; hiking in the forest; kayaking; standing outside on a quiet night, looking at the stars or watching the fireflies):

_____

_____

_____

_____

Times when you're in yellow (e.g., being cut off in traffic; walking alone in the dark; unexpectedly hearing a loud noise; having to do something outside my comfort zone like public speaking):

_____

_____

_____

_____

Times when you're in red (e.g., seeing my family; hearing my brother's voice; interacting with aggressive people; hearing someone outside my apartment):

_____

_____

_____

_____

I mentioned that a healthy system moves flexibly between these states, but after experiencing trauma, it's common for the system to remain prepared for danger. In individuals with CPTSD, ANS reactions are often heightened and prolonged because those responses were needed so often during the trauma. So, to protect these individuals, the ANS learned to live in the yellow zone (to detect danger early on) or in the red zone (to avoid or escape from what was happening). The ANS is trained to maintain these responses and will continue to respond this way even when the trauma is over. So, what do you do? How can you train your system out of these responses if they're no longer serving you or probably even hindering you?

In the last part of the activity you just completed ("times when you're in green"), you identified some things you can do to get yourself back into your green zone. Let's look at other ideas for getting you into green.

Getting Back to Green

I mentioned earlier the polyvagal ladder and that we move through these three states in order: we first move through the yellow zone to get to red and, if we're in the red zone, we have to come back down to yellow before we can get to green. In this section, we're going to look at activities you can do if you find yourself in the yellow or red zones, to help you return to green; then we'll look at ways of stimulating your vagus nerve to improve the overall flexibility of your system.

Moving from Red to Yellow

Let's say your ANS neurocepted something as a life threat, you quickly moved through yellow and you're in that flop and drop state, immobilized, and collapsed, and your system has given up—you're in red. The key here is to get you unfrozen, unstuck, and mobilized by bringing energy back to your body. How can you do that? This will be different for everyone (and may even be different for you in different situations), so here are some things to try:

- Grounding exercises: These are exercises that help you get back into your body.

  - Stomp your feet on the floor or clap your hands: notice the sounds and sensations in your body as you do this.

- This is a practice developed by Bodynamic International: As you inhale deeply, press your big toes into the floor. As you exhale even more deeply, press your little toes into the floor (do this several times).

- Look around and say out loud to yourself, "I see the…" and name three things you see. Then move on to three things you feel, three things you hear, and three things you smell.

- Smell a favorite perfume, an essential oil, or whatever else you have available (it's a good idea to consider this before you need it to be sure the scent you choose isn't triggering).

- Dance, stretch, walk, or play.

- Do some intense exercise: run up and down the stairs in your house or apartment building, run around the block, or do jumping jacks.

- If you have a furry friend, pet them, focusing on the softness of their fur.

Add other ideas you know work for you, or that you're willing to try, here:

_____

_____

_____

_____

_____

_____

_____

Moving from Yellow to Green

According to Dana (2018), it takes twenty minutes to move back into the green zone when we've been in full sympathetic activation (yellow). Whether you've started in yellow, or you've made your way back to yellow from red, you still need to use skills to get you back to green. Here are some ideas:

- Forward bend (Van Dijk 2022): bend over as though you're trying to touch your toes. When we're in a position with our head below our heart, our PNS becomes activated, helping us move out of sympathetic arousal.

- Some people roll their eyes when we talk about the importance of breathing exercises, but you can't dispute the science and we know that making your exhale longer than your inhale also activates the PNS—this is the DBT skill of paced breathing (Linehan 2014). To do this, count (in your head) as you inhale. If you get to four as you inhale, make sure you exhale at least to five. You'll usually find that your breath will naturally slow as you do this, which has a further calming effect. For a double whammy to the PNS, you can also combine this with a forward bend.

- Vocalize: the vagus nerve is connected to our vocal cords, so singing, humming, chanting, or gargling can also help you come back down to your green zone.

Add other ideas you know work for you, or that you're willing to try, here:

_____

_____

_____

_____

_____

_____

A Note About Panic Attacks

Many people who have CPTSD experience panic attacks If this is you, here's some helpful information.

What Is a Panic Attack?

Panic attacks can be scary: Your ANS neurocepts something in the environment as dangerous, catapulting you into sympathetic arousal (big-time yellow zone!), causing all sorts of physical sensations: your breathing is out of control, your blood pressure goes through the roof, you might experience chest pains, dizziness, lightheadedness, nausea, narrowing of your vision…These episodes can be so frightening, you might believe you're going to die, pass out, or "go crazy." Rest assured: you're not dying, you're not going crazy, and you're more than likely not going to pass out (although it's certainly okay to sit down just in case, especially if you've fainted before).

While there are often triggers for panic attacks that can be addressed to help reduce them, and you can learn other skills to manage them more effectively, many people don't realize that the way you breathe is also typically a contributing factor.

Subtle Hyperventilation

While this will depend on different factors, a healthy adult should be inhaling twelve to twenty breaths per minute; if you're inhaling more than this, you're hyperventilating. *Hyperventilation* occurs when you have too much oxygen in your lungs. Symptoms of hyperventilation include dizziness, lightheadedness, shortness of breath, chest pain, rapid heartbeat, numbness or tingling around the mouth or in the hands and arms, dry mouth, and "the little black fuzzies" or other vision changes. While hyperventilation is often brought on by anxiety, the symptoms of overbreathing often increase anxiety, leading to more hyperventilation, and so on.

What to Do About It

People often tell me they try to "deep breathe" when they're having a panic attack. If you're hyperventilating, chances are you're making things worse for yourself by breathing deeply because you're maintaining excess oxygen in your system. So, instead of *deep* breathing, breathe as normally as possible while covering your nose and mouth. You may have seen people in movies use a paper bag when they're hyperventilating. You can do that if you'd like, but it's not necessary—you can use your hands, a cloth, or a towel (face masks will work too!). The key is to cover your nose and mouth so you're breathing recycled air, which contains less oxygen. When you're breathing as normally as possible, those symptoms should begin to subside after a few moments.

The key to keeping hyperventilation at bay in the long run, however, *is* deep breathing—you need to train your body to inhale, slowly and deeply, twelve to twenty times per minute.

*If you experience chest pains, please be sure to speak with your doctor.

The key when we're in red is to increase arousal to get out of that shutdown state. When we're in yellow, we want to reduce arousal to return to calm. You can, of course, try all the activities I've mentioned to help you get back to your green zone regardless of what zone you're starting from. The idea here is for you to have as many options as possible to help you get back to green; you'll also see more ideas to help with this in the second part of this book. Before we move on, let's look at a few more activities that can help you get to and stay in your green zone.

Coregulation

As human beings, we're programmed to seek connection with others, but it's important for us to be aware that the people we surround ourselves with influence our nervous system. *Coregulating* in Polyvagal Theory refers to the idea that our ANS sends cues of safety or danger to the people around us, just as others' systems affect our own. When we're with someone calm, their ANS will help us join them in the green zone (and, of course, this works both ways: when someone else is dysregulated and we can be a calm presence with them, our ANS will help them come back to green). And keep in mind that all mammals have nervous systems, so you can also coregulate with your dog or cat!

Who do you have in your life that's typically a soothing presence and helps you get back to your green zone? Make some notes here about how you coregulate already, and what you can do to practice this:

_____

_____

_____

_____

Stimulating Your Vagus Nerve

Let's finish off by looking at some general ways of exercising your green muscles. Remember that Polyvagal Theory has only been around since the 1990s, so we don't have a lot of research yet on the connection between the vagus nerve and ways of strengthening it, but here are some things you can try.

Mindfulness Meditation

You'll be learning more about mindfulness in chapter five, but I'll mention here that mindfulness can increase heart rate variability, or HRV (Telles et al. 2005), which is one measure of vagal tone (you might already be familiar with HRV as many wearable "smart devices" nowadays measure it). Generally, higher HRV indicates a stronger vagus nerve. So, when you practice mindfulness, you're working your vagus nerve and increasing your ability to move more flexibly between zones.

Exercise

Given how helpful and healthy we know exercise is, it shouldn't be surprising that we do have research showing that physical exercise stimulates the vagus nerve (Bonaz et al. 2017). It doesn't have to be intense or lengthy periods of exercise—if you're not exercising at all, start by taking slow, short walks, or even doing some light stretching. Just move your body.

Cold Water Immersion

If you're on any kind of social media, you've likely seen videos of people climbing into tubs of ice water or jumping into freezing cold lakes. While often this is just for fun (or TikTok), there are also benefits to immersing yourself in cold water—if you do it properly and safely! Research shows that one benefit of cold water immersion is increased HRV, although there is still debate about how cold the water should be and how long you should submerse yourself. If you'd like to experiment, in the last ten to twenty seconds of your shower, reduce the temperature of the water as low as you can tolerate. You can build your tolerance from there (please check with your doctor first if you have any physical health conditions!).

Massage

Massage is another way to stimulate the vagus nerve. Mindful contact with another person is a way of coregulating (if the person giving the massage is also regulated) and generates feel-good chemicals in the brain. If you don't have anyone to give you a massage, or if that's just not comfortable for you, you can also massage your own muscles.

Wrapping Up

In this chapter, you've learned about the ANS and how it's constantly scanning for danger to keep you safe. You've also learned in this chapter that having a healthy ANS isn't about being calm all the time; remember, our system is meant to help us survive, so we don't want it offline altogether! Instead, we want to have a flexible and resilient system that's able to accurately assess safety and danger and respond to those cues appropriately.

One of the most important lessons I hope you've learned in this chapter is that we don't get to choose how our system responds—our ANS chooses for us based on our chances of survival. When your system moves into yellow, it does so because it detects a chance of escape, but when it neurocepts that there's no possibility of surviving by fighting, fleeing, or freezing, the ANS will move you into red, where you can escape the pain differently—for instance, through dissociation.

In the next chapter, we're moving into part two of the book and we'll start to look at other means of survival you might be using that are likely doing you more harm than good, and skills to help you start to move away from these unhealthy ways of coping.

Part II

CHAPTER FOUR

Distress Tolerance Skills

You've learned a lot in part one of this book about the effects of trauma, including its effects on the ANS, and dissociation. Remembering there are reasonable (trauma-related!) explanations for these experiences can help reduce your fear of them. But because the emotions and distressing sensations can be so painful, frightening, and disruptive to daily life, it's not uncommon for people to turn to unhealthy behaviors to cope. This might help in the short term, but it creates a vicious cycle as you come to rely on those unhealthy coping mechanisms to avoid certain experiences.

In this chapter, we'll look at some of those unhealthy means of coping (what we'll call *target behaviors*) and the cycle of reinforcement that keeps you going back to those behaviors even when you know they're doing you more harm than good. Then we'll look at healthier ways of managing distress.

Activity: The Development of Target Behaviors

As you've been learning, the consequences of trauma are many: painful emotions; memories and flash-backs; negative beliefs about yourself; dissociation; distressing physical sensations; and so on. Take a moment to consider how you've tried to avoid or escape from reminders of the trauma or distressing symptoms. Keep in mind that many of these behaviors aren't problematic in and of themselves but can become unhealthy when used excessively or to avoid. Following are some common examples—put a check beside the ones you've used to cope in the last three months:

☐ Drinking alcohol or using drugs

☐ Lashing out at others

☐ Sleeping

☐ Playing video games

☐ Using social media

☐ Gambling

☐ Spending

☐ Restricting food

☐ Purging after eating (e.g., vomiting, using laxatives, overexercising)

☐ Overeating

☐ Self-harming

☐ Thinking about or trying to kill yourself

☐ Engaging in unsafe sexual practices (e.g., having unprotected sex with people you don't know)

☐ Engaging in obsessive thinking or compulsive behaviors (e.g., cleaning, handwashing, counting)

☐ Ruminating (excessive worrying, dwelling, rehashing)

☐ People pleasing

☐ Working excessively

Add any other behaviors you've used in problematic ways here:

_____

_____

What was it like for you to consider this? Perhaps you hadn't realized something you were doing was problematic. Maybe you're still not sure. Or you may already be very aware of your target behaviors. Write your thoughts here:

_____

_____

_____

_____

If you're not sure if you've been engaging in any target behaviors, you might want to ask someone you trust for their perspective or consider feedback you've already received from the people you care about. This might be difficult for you to acknowledge, but the first step in making any change is facing reality as it is.

You began learning about parts of self in chapter two, and as we'll discuss in chapter seven, target behaviors such as those I've just listed are often parts' ways of protecting you. So, not only are these behaviors understandable but we also need to acknowledge they've likely helped you survive at times. Once the trauma is over, however, you need to find healthier ways of managing. Before we look at how to do that, let's first look at something else that will help you to understand these behaviors: the cycle of reinforcement.

The Cycle of Reinforcement

Once you're more aware of your target behaviors, it'll be helpful for you to understand how these behaviors keep you stuck in a vicious pattern of avoidance. I call this the *cycle of reinforcement*. Reinforcement is when something happens after you've engaged in a behavior that makes it more likely you'll engage in the behavior again in the future. *Positive reinforcement* is when something perceived as rewarding happens after a behavior (for instance, winning Employee of the Month makes that employee continue to work hard). *Negative reinforcement* is when something aversive (like a painful emotion, memory, thought, or physical sensation) is *removed* as a result of the behavior. For example, you're having distressing thoughts and memories about a past trauma, so you throw yourself into work to not think about it, reducing your anxiety.

One of the problems with unhealthy coping mechanisms, however, is that the relief is always temporary; at some point, you have to return to the problematic behavior to get more relief. Essentially, you train yourself to believe you can't tolerate the painful experiences. Does this sound familiar? Keep in mind you may not have made a conscious choice to turn to these behaviors. You may have learned unconsciously that thinking about suicide, for example, takes your mind off memories of your past traumas, reducing your pain (negative reinforcement). By the way, we can also see suicidal thinking as a part trying to protect you from pain; in Polyvagal terms, your ANS moves you from yellow to red when it neurocepts (perhaps inaccurately) that there is life threat you can't escape.

Let's get you thinking about how this pattern might fit for you in the following activity.

Activity: Identifying Your Cycle of Reinforcement

Do your best to answer the following questions about your target behaviors (if you've identified more than one, I'd suggest you consider these one at a time to prevent yourself from becoming overwhelmed). If you find yourself struggling with these questions, try to start becoming aware of your patterns and return to this activity when you have more information.

1. Which target behavior are you going to address (first)?

    _____

2. What do you know about when the urge to engage in this behavior arises? For example, does it come up at a certain time of day or day of the week? Is it related to certain people? Does it arise when you're struggling with internal triggers like memories or panic attacks?

    _____

    _____

    _____

3. What does the behavior do for you? Here are some examples: drinking alcohol before you talk to your ex-partner helps you stand up to them (positively reinforcing); lashing out at others gives you a sense of control (positively reinforcing) or keeps others from getting close to you (possibly negatively reinforcing, if this reduces anxiety about others getting close to you).

Learning healthy coping skills—which we'll look at shortly—will help you replace these unhealthy ways of coping. Now let's help you decide if you want to change this behavior by furthering your understanding of it.

Cost-Benefit Analysis

You might already have a thorough understanding of the consequences of this target behavior, but I find that, while people are often familiar with the negative consequences the behavior carries with it, they often haven't thought about the positives. In my experience, if a behavior doesn't benefit us in some way, we wouldn't still be doing it, so it can help to figure out what's maintaining it. This is where a cost-benefit analysis based on the DBT Pros and Cons skill (Linehan 2014) can be helpful, having you identify the positive and negative consequences of engaging in the behavior and the positive and negative consequences of *not* engaging in it. Rating each pro and con from 0 (not important at all) to 5 (most important) can help you feel the weight of each response, rather than relying on how many responses are in each category to help you see your responses in a more objective light. Let's look at a cost-benefit analysis completed on the target behavior of "using work to avoid."

Benefits of Target Behavior: Using Work to Avoid

4/5—It helps me feel in control.

4/5—It reduces my anxiety.

5/5—Working hard makes me feel good about myself.

Total: 13

Costs of Target Behavior: Using Work to Avoid

5/5—It leads to exhaustion.

5/5—I don't get to spend much time with my children.

5/5—It prevents me from creating healthy relationships with others.

2/5—I don't get to do things I enjoy, like traveling.

Total: 17

Benefits of Healthy Coping: Not Using Work to Avoid

5/5—My relationships with my children would improve.

5/5—I'd have more time for romantic relationships and friendships.

4/5—I'll have to learn to deal with my anxiety in healthier ways.

5/5—I'm no longer letting my past control me.

Total: 19

Costs of Healthy Coping: Not Using Work to Avoid

4/5—I'll have to learn to deal with my anxiety in healthier ways.

2/5—My boss won't like it!

4/5—I won't have an excuse not to meet new people!

Total: 10

Notice that doing an analysis like this has you thinking about the target behavior from as many different angles as possible. It also has you score each cost and benefit so you can compare the numerical value of stopping the behavior versus not stopping, which often brings more clarity.

As you can see in this example, the benefits of stopping the behavior outweigh the costs. Most often, completing a cost-benefit analysis helps you see what the wisest course of action is; however, you may find there are times when you can't think of reasons to learn new ways of coping because your old, unhealthy patterns are too difficult to give up. When this happens, one option is to ask the people who care about you for help. They'll likely be able to provide additional reasons to work on reducing or eliminating the behavior.

Now it's your turn to consider one of your target behaviors in the blank cost-benefit analysis provided.

Activity: Cost-Benefit Analysis

Benefits of Target Behavior: _____

_____/5—_____

_____/5—_____

_____/5—_____

_____/5—_____

_____/5—_____

Total: _____

Costs of Target Behavior: _____

_____/5—_____

_____/5—_____

_____/5—_____

_____/5—_____

_____/5—_____

Total: _____

Benefits of Healthy Coping: Not _____

_____/5—_____

_____/5—_____

_____/5—_____

_____/5—_____

_____/5—_____

Total: _____

Costs of Healthy Coping: Not _____

_____/5—_____

_____/5—_____

_____/5—_____

_____/5—_____

_____/5—_____

Total: _____

It's usually most effective if you do your analysis over a few days to ensure you're considering the costs and benefits of the behavior from your wise self (more about how to get to this wise place in the next chapter!). Take your time, and when you're ready to start looking at other behaviors, you'll be able to access this handout online.

Once you've decided on the target behaviors you'd like to change, you'll want to use the skills outlined in the rest of this chapter to help you not act on urges when they arise. It's often difficult to eliminate unhealthy behaviors, especially if you've habitually turned to them to manage trauma-related symptoms; rest assured, there are many techniques we'll be looking at in this chapter (and throughout the book) that will help you not act on those urges. To start, we'll look at some distress tolerance skills (Linehan 2014), which help us learn to tolerate the distress we're experiencing and resist the urge to avoid it through problematic behaviors.

Changing Your Body Chemistry

These skills have become some of my favorites because they're so effective at quickly regulating emotions; the hardest thing about them is to remember to use them when emotions start to feel out of control.

Stick Your Face in Cold Water

In the last chapter, you learned about cold water immersion to stimulate the vagus nerve. This skill, known in DBT as "tipping the temperature of your face with cold water," also uses cold water, but in a different way, and this skill comes with a caution (Linehan 2014): If you have a heart condition, low blood pressure, take beta blockers (a medication used to treat heart or blood pressure problems), or have anorexia or bulimia, move on to the next skill as this one can lead to a rapid decrease in your heart rate, causing you to faint. If this doesn't apply to you, read on!

When emotions start to intensify—or are already intense—go to the nearest sink and fill it with cold water (you can also use a large bowl or a bucket if that's easier). Stick your face in the cold water for twenty to thirty seconds (if you can't hold your breath that long, come up for a breath and repeat if necessary). The combination of cold water, tipping yourself over, and holding your breath tricks the body into thinking it's underwater and activates the *mammalian dive reflex*. This is a reflex that all mammals have: when submerged in water, our body redirects blood flow from our extremities to our heart and brain and lowers blood pressure, helping to regulate emotions—fast!

If you can't use cold water for whatever reason, there are other options (starting with the temperature of the water, although cold water is most effective). The following skills involve ways to activate the PNS. Remember, this is the "rest and digest" system that helps us decrease arousal, so having more ways to get there will be helpful.

Forward Bend

I introduced this skill in chapter three, but it's so effective, it bears mentioning again. Whenever our body is in a position in which our head is below our heart, our PNS is activated. So, bending over as though you're trying to touch your toes or sitting with your head between your knees (also for twenty to thirty seconds if that's tolerable) will help put the brakes on when emotions start to intensify. This is a good option if you can't use cold water; but to make it even more effective, you could put an ice pack over your eyes and hold your breath—a modified version of sticking your face in cold water (but if using cold, the same caution applies as with the cold water skill).

Intense Exercise

Intense exercise boosts certain chemicals in the brain, reducing emotional pain and improving our mood and ability to regulate emotions. So, if you're stressed out and emotions are beginning to overwhelm you, do some jumping jacks or lunges, go for a run or brisk walk, or run up and down the stairs or around the block. This is also a good skill if you're in the red zone and need strategies to increase your arousal to get you out of that shutdown mode.

Suck on Lemons!

Not actually, unless you love lemons! But the point here is that we can also activate the rest and digest PNS by generating saliva—so, yes, sucking on lemons will do it. But so will other things: for example, if I think the words *salt and vinegar* or *dill pickle*, my mouth starts to water. Consider what does this for you or go out and buy some tart candy to suck on.

Try each of these skills to see how they feel for you ahead of time, and then do your best to use them when emotions start to intensify; they won't solve the problem, of course, but they will help reduce the intensity of emotions so you can respond to uncomfortable experiences in a healthier, more adaptive way.

Your List

You may be using some of these skills (or other skills that change your body's chemistry) already. Make a list of any skills you're using already, and the ones you're willing to try here:

_____

_____

_____

_____

_____

_____

_____

_____

RESISTTing the Urge

Regulating your emotions is usually only the first step; to prevent yourself from getting stuck in a loop where they start to intensify once more, you'll often need to figure out what to do next. Let's look at these skills using the acronym RESISTT (Van Dijk 2013):

R: Reframe

E: Engage in an activity

S: Do something for someone else

I: Experience intense sensations

S: Shut it out

T: Think neutral thoughts

T: Take a break

<u>R</u>: Reframe

Learning to think about situations from a different perspective can help reduce emotional pain. There are lots of ways to do this; here are some for you to consider:

- "Find the silver lining": This doesn't mean you tell yourself to suck it up and get over it! It's important to acknowledge the pain you're in. But trying to see something positive in the difficult experience you're facing can make a situation more bearable. For instance, one of my clients was making the difficult decision to take a leave from her job. She didn't want to, but given her ongoing mental health struggles, she knew she wasn't managing work well. Instead of focusing on this as a failure, she reframed it by considering how she would spend her time off: "It sucks that I have to take a leave from work, but my full-time job now is recovering from my eating disorder and doing the trauma work I need to do."

- In DBT, we have another way of reframing called *comparisons* (Linehan 2014). Here are some examples:

- Compare yourself to someone else who isn't coping as well as you are. This doesn't mean judging them but shifting your perspective so you can see that, while things are difficult, they could also be worse. For example, "I'm unhappy with my life right now, but I know what I need to change to be healthier; many of my friends have no plans for the future, so I guess I'm actually ahead of the game."

- Compare yourself to a time in your own life when you weren't managing as well as you are now. Again, this is meant to shift your perspective, not to make you feel guilty or shameful about your past: for instance, "I'm struggling right now, but this is the longest I've been able to stay at a job, so I'm making progress."

- Think of a broader situation in the world that you can use as a comparison: "Things are difficult right now, but I live in a country that is free from war; I have stable housing and means of supporting myself; and I have family and friends on whom I can rely."

However you reframe, it's important to validate the pain you're in before shifting your perspective (we'll come back to this skill, known as self-validation, in chapter six).

Of course, it's not at all uncommon for human beings to *catastrophize*, or imagine the worst possible outcome, but it's important to recognize that the way you talk to yourself influences how you feel. Changing your negative thinking about a situation often makes it more tolerable, increasing your chances of getting through it without turning to a target behavior that might make the situation worse. To change negative thinking, write some coping statements you can say to yourself when you're facing a difficult situation to help you manage in healthier ways. Here are some examples:

- *I can bear this; I've done it before.*

- *These feelings are uncomfortable, but I know I'm safe in this moment.*

- *This pain is temporary; it feels awful, but I know I can get through it.*

- *These are just emotions—they will pass.*

If you're struggling to come up with your own statements, feel free to use these examples if they resonate for you or consider what you might say to someone you care about if they were struggling to help you think of things you can say to yourself.

YOUR LIST

You may be using some of these skills (or other skills to reframe) already; make a list of any skills you're using already, and the ones you're willing to try here:

_____

_____

_____

_____

_____

_____

_____

<u>E</u>: Engage in an Activity

Engaging in an activity is about distracting yourself so you don't make the situation worse in some way. While distracting is not meant to be used in the long term as it can turn into avoidance, there are certainly times when it can be helpful. Generally, if you're facing a problem that can be solved, and there's something you can do about it right now, solve the problem. If there's nothing you can do to solve the problem, or you can't do anything about it right now, you can distract.

Think about what you do to get your mind off things already that don't have negative consequences: Watch a favorite show? Talk to a friend? Cuddle with a pet? Becoming aware of things you do already is a great starting point; you can brainstorm about what else you can do to distract when you're becoming distressed. Here's a list of healthy coping activities to get you started.

Healthy Coping List

Spend time with your pet: walk, groom, play, or snuggle with them

Look at photographs that bring up pleasurable memories

Write a poem or short story

Sing your favorite song

Put on some upbeat music and dance

Go to a movie

Find a fun new ringtone for your cell

Watch online videos of baby animals

Make your favorite treat or meal

Watch your favorite show

Go to the mall or a park to people-watch

Update your social media status

Do a relaxation exercise

Experiment with different hairstyles

Treat yourself to (or DIY) a manicure or pedicure

Imagine yourself in your favorite place

Play a musical instrument

Learn how to crochet, knit, or do something else new

Journal

Play a sport you enjoy or watch it on TV

Rearrange or organize a room in your house

Do a puzzle

Sit outside in the sunshine

Go play pool or billiards

Fantasize about retirement, finishing school, your next vacation, or something else you're looking forward to

Do some yoga, go for a swim, go to the gym, or do some kind of exercise

Dress up

Go for a drive

Watch a TED Talk

Play an online game you enjoy

Go explore (driving, walking, hiking) an area you're not familiar with

Light some scented candles

Go to the zoo, a petting farm, or an aquarium

Go bowling

Plan or organize an event

Make a plan to improve your health (for example, eating healthier, increasing exercise, taking medications as prescribed, reducing substance use)

Go to a museum or art gallery

Go to a place of worship

Do a chore or run an errand

Go to a greenhouse, an arboretum, or a botanical garden

Volunteer your time

Walk barefoot in the grass

Read funny things online (like funny Autocorrects!)

Look at the stars

Watch funny YouTube videos

Connect with a friend (but don't spend the whole time talking about the situation you're trying to distract from!)

Listen to some upbeat music

Read a book or magazine

Do some research on something you find interesting

Take a bubble bath

Make a list of:

- ◆ countries you'd like to visit

- ◆ famous people (past or present) you'd like to meet

- ◆ sights you'd most like to see

- ◆ three questions you'd ask someone you could bring back to life

Draw, paint, doodle, or do a craft you enjoy

Play a board game with someone

Google "ways to distract" or "pleasant activities" and add ideas to your list!

YOUR LIST

You may be using some of these skills (or other skills to distract) already; make a list of any skills you're using already, and the ones you're willing to try here:

_____   _____

_____   _____

_____   _____

_____   _____

_____   _____

<u>S</u>: Do Something for Someone Else

Are there things you do already that have you focus on someone else to get your mind off your own stuff? Read the following ideas to help you come up with more:

Shovel your neighbor's snow, rake their leaves, or cut their grass.

Bake some cookies and drop them off to a friend.

Do some volunteer work at a local animal shelter or food bank.

Offer to take care of your friend's children for a few hours.

Send someone a card to let them know you're thinking of them.

Of course, your choice of activities will depend on your current circumstances: if you're stuck in your yellow zone having panic attacks, or a fearful part is running the show, it likely won't be comfortable for you to take care of your friend's children; if you're dissociating or you can't focus because of the panic, it might not even be safe. This is one reason it's helpful to have many options for skills: if now isn't the right time to babysit your friend's children, no problem—you've got lots of other skills to choose from.

YOUR LIST

You may be using some of these skills (or other skills involving doing something for someone else) already; make a list of any skills you're using already, and the ones you're willing to try here:

_____   _____

_____   _____

_____   _____

_____   _____

_____   _____

I: Experience Intense Sensations

Another set of skills that are effective in getting us through difficult situations without making things worse involves considering what's soothing for your senses. Keep in mind the more intensely you experience the sensation, the more it will help get your mind off the urges and emotions. Here are some examples:

SIGHT

Look at pictures of people or pets you love; drive or walk to a place where you can observe nature; go to an art gallery; buy a bouquet of flowers or one flower; or pick some wildflowers and put them somewhere you'll see them often.

SOUND

Listen to soothing music; have someone you care about record a message so you can hear their voice; listen to sounds of nature that are soothing for you, like waves, rain, crickets, or a thunderstorm.

TOUCH

Hug someone; put clean sheets on your bed and enjoy the feel as you slide between them; sit by a fire or in the sun and feel the warmth of it.

TASTE

Treat yourself to your favorite meal or snack; suck on a favorite flavored candy; drink an herbal tea.

SMELL

Use some aromatherapy (lavender, for example, is calming); put on a favorite perfume, cologne, or body lotion; or stop and smell the roses! Keep in mind that our memory for scent is the strongest of all our senses, so it's a good idea to choose smells when you're not in crisis so you can be sure the scents you choose won't trigger you further.

YOUR LIST

You may be using some of these skills (or other skills to soothe your senses) already; make a list of any skills you're using already, and the ones you're willing to try here:

_____   _____

_____   _____

_____   _____

_____   _____

_____   _____

By the way: self-soothing is good self-care, so unlike the other skills in this section, I would encourage you to use these skills on a regular basis!

S: Shut It Out

Another strategy we can use to get our mind off a distressing experience is to "shut it out." The idea here is not to avoid the experience but to temporarily set it aside to be considered or worked with later. Let me emphasize that what we're shutting out is the event itself, not emotions, and not parts! Let's look at some ways to do this.

CREATE A CONTAINER

This is an imaginal exercise that has you creating a container in which to place a distressing experience. Remember that this is meant to be temporary, which means you put things into your container and you're also able to take them back out again. We also want it to be what I refer to as a *neutral* container—in other words, it's not a garbage bin but it also doesn't have to be an extravagantly furnished room. Here are some examples: a safe, filing cabinet, magical pouch, closet, storage container, or chest. I encourage my clients to create some kind of locking mechanism to provide an extra sense of control, but do what feels best for you. What comes to mind as you read this?

Activity: Using Your Container

In this activity, you'll practice using your imaginal container, but if you struggle with this, you can move on to the next section where I'll provide suggestions for using a concrete container.

Closing your eyes, envision your container.

Tip: If you struggle to visualize, you can look at something real that you can base your imaginal container on. Then, when I say "imagine" or "visualize," see if you can *experience* or *sense* your container rather than seeing it. Describe the container in as much detail as you can: What color is it? How big is it? Is it textured? Does it lock? Make some notes about your container here; you can also give it a name (such as "The Vault"), or you can draw a picture of it:

_____

_____

_____

_____

Once you have a good sense of your container, think of a recent situation that was uncomfortable (perhaps irritating, or mildly anxiety-provoking). It's best not to start with a high level of discomfort, so aim for perhaps a 2 or 3 on a scale from 0 (no disturbance) to 10 (the highest disturbance you can imagine). See if you can feel the emotion as you recall the situation. Now, envision or feel yourself placing that experience into your container (for example, if you're worrying about a problem you had with your boss, you might put your boss into the container). Take a moment to really get a sense of containing the problem. When you're done, re-rate the level of disturbance from 0 to 10; you'll hopefully find that it's decreased. As you get more comfortable with your container, you'll be able to use it with more distressing experiences as well.

GET CONCRETE

You can also turn this into a more concrete exercise by writing out a title for the uncomfortable experience on a piece of paper (to return to the example of your boss, you might write your boss's name or a description of the problem, such as "No bonus at work this year"). Then put the paper into a physical container (consider putting this somewhere you won't constantly see it to help you let go of the experience that's bothering you).

YOUR LIST

You may be using some of these skills (or other skills to shut it out) already; make a list of any skills you're using already, and the ones you're willing to try here:

_____   _____

_____   _____

_____   _____

_____   _____

_____   _____

T: Think Neutral Thoughts

If you've ever been given the advice, "count to ten when you're feeling angry," that's what this skill is about. It's difficult to continue feeling an emotion while we're focusing on neutral thoughts. Here are some other examples:

Sing your favorite song

Repeat a calming or soothing mantra (such as *I am safe* or *Come back to the present*)

Count backward from 100 by 3s

Look at a picture and name the objects you see

Go through the alphabet and list an animal that starts with each letter

YOUR LIST

You may be using some of these skills (or other skills to distract with neutral thoughts) already; make a list of any skills you're using already, and the ones you're willing to try here:

_____   _____

_____   _____

_____   _____

_____   _____

_____   _____

T: Take a Break

Taking a break when emotions are intense and you're noticing yourself moving up the polyvagal ladder can help you get through a difficult time without turning to target behaviors. Read the following examples and consider what this might look like for you:

- Go for a walk or drive to clear your head and reduce feelings of overwhelm

- Order takeout instead of having to cook and clean up

- Take a day off work and stay in your pajamas all day watching movies

- Find a last-minute vacation somewhere: book a cottage, go camping, or go stay with a friend

- Do a mindfulness practice (we'll be looking at mindfulness in the next chapter, if this is new to you), a relaxation exercise, some yoga, or something else that helps you feel calmer or at peace, such as the calm place (coming up next!)

Just be sure there are no long-term consequences if you're taking a break—it can't interfere with your responsibilities or long-term goals. Keep in mind that breaks, used too often, can also turn into avoidance; they should be used sparingly, but they can be invaluable.

Activity: Creating a Calm Place

Sometimes you can't physically get away from a problematic situation, but you can create a place in your mind to help you feel calmer—this is the purpose of the calm place (or healing place, peaceful place—use whatever words fit best for you). Take a moment to think of a place that's calming for you: this can be a place you've been, like a favorite vacation spot or hiking trail or it can be a fictional place, like a castle in the clouds (as with the container, if you struggle to visualize, you can look at a photograph or draw a picture of a place you'd like to be). Closing your eyes if that's comfortable, do your best to really *feel* the place as you visit it—notice any sights, smells, sounds, and anything you feel physically or emotionally while you're in your calm place.

Write the name of your calm place here: _____

_____

Now, let's practice. Recall a situation you encountered that was frustrating or annoying—again on a scale from 0 (neutral) to 10 (the most disturbance imaginable), aim for about 2 or 3. Once you've brought the situation to mind and the disturbance associated with it, bring to mind your calm place once more—recall the name you gave it and everything associated with it, and do your best to experience it in as much detail as possible. Notice if the disturbance you're recalling decreases as you experience the peacefulness of that place. If it does, wonderful! Be sure to use your calm place in times of distress to help you manage these emotions. You might also use your container to put something disturbing away before you go to your calm place. If you didn't find your disturbance went down, don't worry—it's not uncommon for people with CPTSD to struggle with shifting from a painful to a calmer state; if that's the case, you've learned something about yourself and this is something you'll need to practice.

YOUR LIST

You may be using some of these skills (or other skills to take a break) already; make a list of any skills you're using already, and the ones you're willing to try here:

_____   _____   _____

_____   _____   _____

We all know how hard it can be to think straight when we get into crisis and emotions start to get intense; having your list of distress tolerance skills takes the thinking out of the equation, making you less likely to engage in a target behavior. So, before you finish with this chapter, I'd suggest that you go back through all the skills you've listed in each section—the ones you use already, and the ones you're willing to try—and write them down on a separate piece of paper or put them in your phone. This is your list of distress tolerance skills that you'll want to have easy access to when things get difficult so you don't have to think about what you can do to get through the crisis—you can just pull out your list and it'll tell you what to do. You can add to this list as you continue to work your way through this book and learn new skills to use when things get tough.

Wrapping Up

These skills are just the start, meant to replace target behaviors you've been turning to and to help you manage intense emotions when they arise. In other words, these skills are meant to help increase safety and stability so you'll be able to move on to stage two (trauma resolution)—if you choose—which will result in less need for distress tolerance skills over time, as the past will no longer be present in your daily life.

In the next chapter, we'll begin looking at the skills that are meant to be used on a more regular basis to help you manage emotions more effectively, beginning with the skill of mindfulness.

CHAPTER FIVE

Mindfulness Skills

In the last chapter, we shifted our focus from learning about trauma to learning skills to help you manage the fallout of trauma. As you learned in chapter one, emotion dysregulation is one symptom of CPTSD, which is why we started with these skills to help you manage emotions more effectively. If you recall, however, distress tolerance skills aren't meant to be your go-to in the long term as that can easily turn into avoidance. This is where other DBT skills come in, starting with mindfulness, which is a core DBT skill and will be helpful in your recovery from trauma in many ways.

In this chapter, you'll learn what mindfulness is and how it will be helpful. Then we'll return to look more closely at parts of self (introduced in chapter two), with the help of a DBT skill known as *states of mind*.

Mindfulness: What It Is

You're out for a walk on a sunny day, the flowers are blooming, but you're feeling angry as you dwell on a fight you had with your friend. Or you're having a panic attack as you're stuck in the past reliving your trauma, or perhaps you're not feeling anything as you're in a dissociative trance. These are examples of mind*less*ness, when our attention is divided, we're not fully in the present moment (or, in the case of trance, we're not *at all* in the present moment), and we're caught up in judgments of ourselves, situations, or others.

Mindfulness, in contrast, involves doing one thing at a time, in the present moment, with our full attention, and with acceptance. When we're being mindful, we've taken ourselves off automatic pilot, we're engaged with what we're doing in this moment (our mind still wanders, but we notice that and come back to the present), and we're open, curious, and accepting of whatever we're experiencing— both within ourselves and in the world around us. Let's look at *why* you would want to do this before we delve into the *how*.

Mindfulness Increases Self-Awareness

When we're being mindful, we're living more in the present, so when emotions, thoughts, physical sensations, and urges arise, we'll be more aware of them because we're paying attention. And when we're being mindful, we're more accepting of our experiences, meaning we'll be less likely to avoid or ignore unpleasant experiences. How is this helpful?

Awareness of Emotions

Quite often, trauma teaches people that emotions are not to be expressed and are safer to be avoided. Consider a child who's expressing frustration, crying because they're sad or anxious, or being playful, but their behavior is interpreted by an abusive parent as "bad" and in need of punishment—for this child, expressing emotions can be downright dangerous. Pushing emotions away becomes the safest course for the child, but as an adult, this (often unconscious) avoidance is no longer helpful and actually causes more problems (for example, they're not able to express anger, so resentment builds and they blow up or they end up taking it out on themselves through self-harm or other means).

Being aware of our emotions is important for many reasons: for instance, psychiatrist Dan Siegel reminds us that, in order to tame emotions, we have to be able to name them (2014). In other words, if we can't recognize the emotion we're feeling, we won't be as effective at taming it through skills such as problem-solving or self-validation (a skill we'll look at in the next chapter).

Are you able to accurately name your emotions? Or do you use vague language like, "upset" or "bad"? When asked how you feel, do you find yourself describing thoughts instead (for example, "I feel like it's not fair that we're not getting a bonus at work this year!")? Make some notes about your thoughts here:

_____

_____

_____

_____

You'll have the opportunity to consider this in chapter six, and if you find this is an area where you struggle, I'll have some tools to help. For now, know that mindfulness will help you accurately label your emotions as you become more in tune with and accepting of these and the related internal experiences.

Awareness of Triggers

A *trigger* is something in the present that reminds us (consciously or otherwise) of an unresolved trauma. A trigger can take any form: it might be a person who reminds us of someone associated with negative past experiences; it could be a sensation (I learned through doing my own work that having water leak into my mask while scuba diving was triggering an unconscious memory of a near-drowning experience when I was a toddler—who knew?). A trigger could be a song on the radio; a time of day (such as someone who becomes anxious at night, when the sexual abuse they experienced as a child would take place); or a time of year (like birthdays or anniversaries). Smells are also common triggers, such as the smell of the cologne a perpetrator wore or the smell of cookies your abusive mother used to bake. Triggers can be internal (things happening within you, like physical sensations, self-talk, and memories) or external (things happening in your environment, such as the sound of someone walking down the hallway in your house). You may not be aware of your triggers yet, but take a moment to consider what you do know and make some notes here:

_____

_____

_____

_____

In response to the trigger, you become *triggered*—up the polyvagal ladder you go, and on come your defense systems—your parts become activated, and you may find yourself reacting in ways similar to how you reacted during the original trauma (and remember, even if you don't have conscious recall for the event, your body remembers). Janina Fisher notes that, "When we remember a traumatic event, or when we are triggered by some small cue in the here and now, our bodies auto-matically begin to mobilize for danger, not knowing that we are remembering threat rather than being threatened now" (Fisher 2017, 96). This is because the amygdala—the part of the brain that responds to stress and triggers our active defenses—isn't able to differentiate between past and present, so we feel as though the danger is happening *now.*

Flashbacks and dissociation are obvious signs of being triggered, but signs can also be subtler, such as:

- Feeling like you're not in control of your reaction

- Having a reaction that seems more intense than what's warranted by the situation

- Reacting differently from how you would usually react

- Becoming stuck in your reaction, unable to step back and access your internal wisdom

- Feeling as though you're "not yourself," as though another part of you has taken over

Consider your experience of being triggered. This may not look the same every time, but you may have noticed some patterns. Write what you know here:

_____

_____

_____

_____

_____

_____

Of course, you may not have this information yet, but others may have helpful observations for you about your triggers and what being triggered looks like for you. If you don't have anyone you can ask about this, or if it's not comfortable to do so, know that mindfulness will help you develop this awareness over time so you can come back to this section later.

Awareness of Early Warning Signs

It can also be helpful to know your early warning signs if you experience dissociation and flashbacks. With practice, people are often able to pick up on something that happens just before they start to dissociate or have a flashback—changes in breathing; things becoming "fuzzy" or "foggy"; or feeling dizzy or lightheaded. Being aware of your polyvagal zones will also be helpful: since dissociation happens in the red zone, when you notice you've moved into yellow (for example, your heart rate and respiration increase), you'll know you're heading into dissociation territory if you don't use skills to get back to green.

Make some notes about what you know about your early warning signs of dissociation or flashbacks, if this applies to you:

_____

_____

_____

_____

_____

_____

_____

_____

Mindfulness Increases Pleasurable Emotions

Approaching life mindfully can have a calming effect on us—when we're mindful, we tend to be less overwhelmed by dividing our attention and multitasking and we judge ourselves less, which spares ourselves painful emotions such as anger and shame. In addition, mindfulness helps us experience more pleasure: it can be easy to miss out on moments of calm or contentment because they're often not as intense as moments of pain. When we're living in the present with acceptance more often, we'll be more in tune with those pleasurable feelings, even if they're not strong or long-lasting.

People sometimes also become fearful of when the other shoe will drop, so to speak: if they feel content, love, or happiness, for instance, they worry about when that emotion will end. This is such a common experience that author Brené Brown (2012) coined the term *foreboding joy* to describe it. Essentially, we chase away the pleasurable emotion by getting caught up in worrying about when it will end. If instead we accept the emotion, notice when we start to worry about the future, and bring ourselves back to this moment, we'll be more able to enjoy the pleasure.

Think about your own experience of pleasurable emotions and make some notes here about what you know:

_____

_____

_____

_____

_____

_____

_____

Mindfulness Helps Us Not Act on Urges

By being more aware of triggers and internal experiences, you can increase your awareness of urges (which consist of emotions, thoughts, and physical sensations), allowing you the choice of acting on the urge or doing something else. That isn't to say that not acting on the urge is easy, but having awareness of urges earlier on will give you more time to make healthier choices like using skills instead.

This list is not exhaustive, but hopefully, you're starting to understand some of the ways mindfulness will be helpful. If we also put all these pieces together, hopefully, you can see that mindfulness will help you learn to observe (rather than react to) your experiences and to describe those experiences nonjudgmentally: this is the basis of parts work, which we'll be looking at in chapter seven.

Write your thoughts here about how you think mindfulness might be helpful for you:

_____

_____

_____

_____

_____

Now, let's look at how to practice.

Mindfulness: How to Do It

One common (mis)understanding of mindfulness is that it involves meditation. While you can practice mindfulness in this way (such as doing a body scan or guided imagery), you don't have to meditate to be mindful. Since meditating can be very difficult, especially when you have a history of trauma, I'm going to start by introducing what we refer to as *informal* mindfulness, which entails living life more mindfully. If you have prior experience with mindfulness meditation (or *formal* mindfulness), I'd invite you to set aside what you know as best as you can and pretend you're learning about mindfulness for the first time.

Four Steps to Mindfulness

When it comes to informal mindfulness, there's an infinite number of ways to practice; you can use the following steps to guide you:

1. Choose the activity you'll do mindfully. For instance, you could read the rest of this page mindfully, pet your dog or cat mindfully, or have a conversation mindfully.

2. Start focusing on the activity. Remember you're doing one thing at a time, so turn your full attention to that one thing. If you're reading this page mindfully, you're just reading:

turn off the television or the music you're listening to, stop petting your dog or cat, and just read.

3. At some point, you'll notice your mind wander…This is normal! The human brain generates thousands of thoughts each day, so it's almost impossible for your brain to *not* wander. Step three is noticing when this happens—oh look, you're no longer completely focused on the words you're reading ("Yes, my mind wanders all the time, I'm barely ever in the present. How am I ever going to be able to do this…" and off you go!). Yes, this is normal.

4. As best as you can, without judging (yourself, others, distractions in your environment, and so on), bring your attention back to the activity you're doing.

Then repeat steps three and four over and over again: Notice when you've wandered, do your best to not judge, and re-focus. And look, there you go again…Notice it, accept, and come back. Don't expect that you won't wander—the point of mindfulness isn't to stay focused but to notice when you've wandered and bring yourself back (without judgment).

Now let's see what it looks like to practice mindfulness formally.

Formal Mindfulness Practice

Remember, it's not essential that you practice mindfulness formally, but these exercises can be very helpful. I'll provide a couple of exercises for you to try throughout this book (refer to the Further Reading section if you're looking for more on this). With a trauma history, however, it's important that you be cautious with formal practices, especially if you tend to dissociate or have flashbacks or intrusive thoughts and memories. Keep practices short (no longer than two minutes to start). Using a timer is a good idea—if you dissociate or have a flashback, the sound of the timer will help bring you back. It's also important to keep your eyes open, as you're much more vulnerable to dissociation and flashbacks with eyes closed. Just be sure to find a place to rest your eyes during the practice that won't be distracting for you.

Let's start with a breathing practice you can do mindfully that will also help regulate emotions by activating your PNS: Paced Breathing.

Activity: Mindfulness with Paced Breathing

This is the skill I introduced in chapter three to help you move from yellow to green, activating your PNS through making your exhale longer than your inhale; let's look at how to turn this into a mindfulness practice by using the four steps:

1. Choose your focus. I've chosen for us—paced breathing. (Here's your reminder to set your timer for two minutes).

2. Start to focus on breathing: inhale, count; exhale, count, and make the exhale longer than your inhale (so if you inhale to four, make sure you exhale at least to five, for instance).

3. Notice when your attention wanders.

4. Gently, without judging, bring your attention back to your breath.

Continue to notice when your mind wanders and bring yourself back without judging. Wandered again? Yep, you're human—accept it and come back to just counting and breathing, until the timer goes off.

When you've finished, consider what this exercise was like for you. Stick to descriptive language, rather than judgments: What did you notice? Any urges—to move around, stop the practice, or anything else? Did you act on the urges, or were you able to just sit with them, returning your attention to your breath? Did you struggle to stay focused? Make some notes here:

_____

_____

_____

_____

_____

If you dissociated or had flashbacks, intrusive thoughts, memories, or images and you had your eyes open during the practice, please don't be discouraged; remember, formal mindfulness can be especially difficult when you have a history of trauma. There are various changes you can make to your practice (such as doing something that doesn't focus on your body or breath and making the practice shorter), but I would suggest you stick to informal practices for now while you use some of the skills you're learning to help you stay grounded. Remember, the goal right now is stability.

In the next section, you'll learn about a DBT skill known as states of mind, which will give you another option for being mindful.

States of Mind

In DBT, we believe everyone has three *states of mind* (Linehan 2014), or different ways of thinking and being in the world: reasoning mind, emotion mind, and wise mind. I've also come to think of these three states as different parts of the self. Let's look at each of these states and learn more about how to access our internal wisdom.

Reasoning Mind

Reasoning mind is the part of us we access when we're using our logical, straightforward, matter-of-fact thinking about something. There's no emotion involved in this state: we're focused on just the facts; if there is emotion, it's minimal and isn't influencing our behavior. For example, when I'm making a grocery list, I'm looking through the cupboards and fridge, writing down the things I need; for me, there's no emotion involved in this (if you have strong emotions, such as anxiety about food and eating, this likely won't be a reasoning mind experience for you—keep in mind that these states will be different for everyone).

Of course, there are times when it's handy to be in our reasoning mind—I don't need emotions getting in the way when I'm making my grocery list. The goal isn't to get rid of this part of ourselves (or any part!) but to be aware of when we're acting from our reasoning, and to be able to get to another state if we recognize that would be helpful.

Think of some times you're in reasoning mind and write them here: _____

_____

_____

_____

Emotion Mind

When we're in emotion mind, we're not just feeling an emotion—we're being controlled by it: for example, avoiding whatever is causing your anxiety or lashing out at people in anger. It's important to recognize that we can also be in emotion mind with pleasurable emotions, like when you get exciting news and you call your friends and family to share it or you post on social media. So, of course, we don't want to get rid of this state either; even when emotions are painful, emotion mind helps us connect and empathize with others when they're in pain, so we need this state. Again, what's important is that we're able to recognize when we're in emotion mind and do something to get ourselves to a more balanced state when we want to or need to.

Think of some times you're in emotion mind and write them here: _____

_____

_____

_____

Recall our discussion of parts from chapter two: many people with a trauma history have developed a personality that has fragmented into one (or more, in DID) normal life part—the part that does what needs to be done, is rational and grounded, and avoids reminders of the trauma—and one or more trauma parts—the parts that hold information related to the trauma and the fear that it will happen again. You can probably easily recognize emotion mind as trauma parts: these are the parts that are related to our defense systems, so they're angry (fight), afraid (flight and freeze), ashamed (submit), and desperate for connection (cry for help). Reasoning mind will also sometimes be related to trauma parts as we avoid or try to ignore emotions out of fear, shame, and so on.

The normal life part is also not integrated, but this part might not be quite as easy to categorize as emotion mind or reasoning mind. I'd suggest that this part might fall into either category, depending on the situation, and probably also depending on your temperament: some people tend to "default" to reasoning mind, and others default to emotion mind. The goal, though, is to have access to your reasoning, your emotions, and all trauma-related material, allowing you to make healthy choices, rather than being driven by fragmented parts of your self. This is where wise mind comes in.

Wise Mind

You've heard me mention this state of mind throughout this book. When we're in *wise mind*, we draw on our logic or reasoning without being controlled by it, we feel our emotions without being taken over by them, and we take into consideration our intuition (which includes past learning experiences, knowledge, and values). Putting these together, we get to a place of *knowing*, deep down and with our entire being, what the wise thing is in this moment.

Let's look at Lincoln's story to help deepen your understanding of these states.

Lincoln's Story

As a child, Lincoln always butted heads with his parents: they saw him as a troublemaker, a bad student who struggled to pass his classes, and who was never able to meet their expectations. He was bullied in school, but his parents told him it was his own fault for not doing more to fit in with the other kids. More than once, his father told him he needed to "stop being so emotional." At the age of fourteen, Lincoln ran away several times and was fighting with his parents so much that they eventually had him put into foster care.

Now, Lincoln is forty-two years old and he's realized that his fear of abandonment (an attach part) drives him to do whatever he can to get people to like him and not leave. This includes ignoring emotions such as resentment when he continuously gives and receives nothing in return— his logic tells him that, if you ask for too much or become too needy, people will leave you (reasoning mind/trauma parts). More than once, he's made up stories about his health so people will spend more time with him (emotion mind/trauma parts).

Wise mind would have Lincoln be aware and accepting of his emotions and behaviors (they make sense given the fact that his parents abandoned him as a child) and working to make healthy changes using skills. The key here is that Lincoln isn't allowing just his reasoning or his emotions to run the show but finds a balance between these two and brings in his intuition—this is his balanced, integrated, wise mind.

When you've experienced complex trauma, wise mind can be difficult to access. But trust me when I say it *is* there within you! Let's look at some skills to help you get there, starting with some concrete lifestyle changes you might choose to make.

Increasing Access to Wise Mind: STRONGR

There are things we all do at times that reduce our ability to access our wise mind; let's look at how to improve your ability to reach that more balanced perspective with the acronym STRONGR (based on Van Dijk 2022):

Sleep (the right amount for you)

Treat physical and emotional health problems

Resist using drugs and alcohol

One thing each day to build mastery

Nutrition (balance it)

Get exercise

Reduce screen time

Sleep

The average adult requires seven to nine hours of sleep each night, but we're all different, and you need to figure out what works best for you. If you're not already aware of how much sleep you need to function ideally, the best way to figure this out is to pay attention to things like how rested you feel upon waking, what your energy level is like, and if you're struggling with cognitive abilities, like concentration and memory. If you're sleeping too much or are regularly sleep-deprived, it will be more difficult to access your wise mind.

Treat Physical and Emotional Health Problems

As you learned in chapter two (remember ACEs?), there are good reasons trauma survivors experience more health problems than those who don't have this history. Since we can't disconnect the body from the mind, it's important to take care of physical health to manage mental health more effectively, whether a chronic condition, like diabetes or fibromyalgia, or an acute illness, like a cold. Physical health problems can make it more difficult to access wise mind, so following your healthcare providers' treatment recommendations is important. Treating mental health problems might include taking medications as prescribed (or using complementary and alternative medicine if that's your preference), seeing a psychotherapist, surrounding yourself with supportive people, or reading books like this one!

Resist Using Drugs and Alcohol

We've already discussed that trauma puts people at risk for substance misuse; substances can also make it more difficult to access your wise mind (and not just at the time of use, but potentially for days after). If you find yourself turning to drugs or alcohol to help you feel better (for example, to avoid emotions, or to help you relax or "unwind"), this may be a problem.

One Thing Each Day to Build Mastery

Building mastery (Linehan 2014) means doing something that gives you a sense of fulfillment, accomplishment, or pride for what you've done. Doing at least one thing daily that builds mastery helps you access your wise mind and in the long run contributes to an increase in self-respect and self-esteem. This will look different for everyone, so consider what you do already that gives you a sense of fulfillment or accomplishment, and what more you could be doing. Examples include going to work, pushing yourself to get out of the house, doing something that you've been avoiding, or trying a new skill.

Nutrition

When your body isn't getting enough nutrients, your mood is likely to be affected—you might experience lower mood, *hanger* (anger related to hunger!), and anxiety—and it will be harder to get to your wise mind. So, it's important that you eat enough (for example, not skipping meals or restricting calories, eating enough nutritious foods), but not too much (for example, by binge-eating, or regularly overeating). It's also helpful to be aware of how much caffeine you're ingesting as this is a stimulant that can contribute to anxiety, anger emotions such as irritability, and poor sleep. Sugar is another substance that can increase emotional instability, as can dehydration. So, being aware of how much sugar you're consuming and whether you're drinking enough liquids will also help you increase access to your wise mind.

Getting Exercise

It's a well-known fact that exercise can help us manage emotions more effectively. Some studies have shown that exercise that increases heart rate is just as effective at reducing depression as antidepressant medication (if we think of depression as being in the red zone, and exercise increases the heart rate moving us back down toward green, this makes sense!). Even if you don't experience depression, exercise can help you manage emotions in healthier ways and increase your access to wise mind.

Reducing Screen Time

Over the last few decades, as technology has changed, people have been looking at screens for longer periods of time. Research shows that excessive screen time has a negative impact on the developing brains of children and adolescents (shocker, right?). While the brain is considered fully developed at about the age of twenty-five and therefore its development isn't affected by technology after that age, social media can also contribute to emotion dysregulation, making it more difficult for us to access our wise mind. The recommendation is that we spend no more than two hours each day using screens recreationally and that we turn technology off sixty minutes before bed.

Activity: Consider How to Get STRONGR

Consider the following questions (adapted from Van Dijk 2022) to help increase your ability to access wise mind.

Sleep

Approximately how many hours of sleep do you get each night? _____

Do you generally feel rested upon waking? _____

Do you usually take a nap? If so, for how long? _____

After you nap, do you usually feel better or worse? _____

Do you ingest substances that might interfere with sleep, such as caffeine or other stimulants (coffee, tea, energy drinks, caffeine pills, diet pills, chocolate)? _____

Based on your answers, and keeping in mind that too much or too little sleep can leave you feeling irritable, lethargic, and sluggish, do you need to increase or decrease the amount of time you're sleeping?

_____

If you've identified this as an area to work on, what's one small step you can take to start working toward that goal? (For example, if you need to increase sleep, you could set a goal to go to bed fifteen minutes earlier tonight, then work your way up, or you might identify needing to reduce caffeine to improve sleep.)

_____

Treat Physical and Emotional Health Problems

Do you have physical or emotional health problems that require medication or other treatment? If so, do you follow your healthcare providers' recommendations for treatment?

_____

_____

If you've identified this as an area to work on, what's one small step you can take to start working toward that goal? (For example, you could learn more about your illness to understand why the treatment is necessary.)

_____

_____

Resist Using Drugs and Alcohol

Do you currently drink alcohol or use drugs (including illicit, prescription, and over-the-counter medications)? If so, what do you use, and how often?

_____

Do you see your use causing problems for you in work, school, relationships, or any other aspect of your life? _____

Has anyone told you your substance use is a problem? _____

When you're using drugs or alcohol, do you tend to do things you later regret? _____

Do you find yourself turning to drugs or alcohol to deal with emotions? _____

If you've identified this as an area to work on, what's one small step you can take to start working toward that goal? (For example, if alcohol is a problem, you could set a goal to drink only one night on the weekend instead of two and decrease your consumption from there. If you don't think this is a problem you can handle on your own, you might set a goal to look into getting help.)

_____

_____

One Thing Each Day to Build Mastery

List at least three things you do to build mastery:

_____

_____

_____

How many days per week do you do an activity that builds mastery? _____

If you've identified this as an area to work on, what's one small step you can take to start working toward that goal? (For example, you might start by making a list of activities you used to do that gave you this feeling.)

_____

_____

Nutrition

Do you eat three healthy meals as well as some snacks each day? _____

Do you find yourself eating just because you have an urge to—maybe out of boredom or due to another uncomfortable emotion? _____

Do you not eat, or purge food (for example, by vomiting, overexercising, or using laxatives) to lose weight or feel more in control? _____

How much caffeine do you ingest each day? _____

How many glasses of water (or other non-caffeinated liquids) do you drink each day? _____

Sometimes, people develop problems with eating for which they need to seek professional help, and trauma is associated with a greater incidence of eating disorders. If you feel you have an eating problem you can't manage on your own, please speak to a healthcare professional. If that's not the case, but you've identified eating as an area to work on, what's one small step you can take to start working toward that goal? (For example, if you currently eat one meal a day, you could set a goal to start eating something small for breakfast and work your way up.)

_____

_____

Getting Exercise

Do you currently do any type of exercise? If so, how often and for how long? _____

If you have any physical health problems, please check with your doctor before you start an exercise routine. If you've identified exercise as an area to work on, what's one small step you can take to start working toward that goal? (For example, if you currently exercise once a week for fifteen minutes, you could increase this to twice a week and work your way up to more.)

_____

_____

Reducing Screen Time

How much time in a day are you looking at a screen, not related to work? (If you're losing time because you're on your phone, that's also important to note here!)

_____

Do you notice painful emotions resulting from your screen use (such as reading about certain topics that bring up strong feelings)? Write your thoughts here:

_____

_____

_____

_____

Do you find your use of screens interfering with your ability to connect with family and friends? (For instance, has anyone commented on how much time you spend on technology? Do you find yourself dividing your attention between talking to your loved ones and looking at your phone?)

_____

Do you use your phone or other screens right up until bedtime? _____

If you've identified screen time as an area you need to work on, what's one small step you can take to start working toward that goal? (For example, if you find yourself on your phone for six hours a day, perhaps you set a goal to shut down technology fifteen minutes before bed and you can work your way up to more.)

_____

_____

It can be easy to overwhelm yourself by taking on too much at once, so if you've identified more than one STRONGR skill to work on, decide what you'd like to work on first and write it here:

_____

_____

_____

_____

_____

Activities to Increase Access to Wise Mind

The STRONGR skills will help you access your wise mind through making concrete lifestyle changes; now, let's look at some specific activities you can do to help you access your wise mind.

Creating a Shortcut

It can be helpful to have a "shortcut," a person who represents wise mind for you. When you're facing a difficult situation, you can draw on this resource to help you get to that more balanced state (for example, one of my clients identified Superman as representing wise mind, so he would ask himself, "What would Superman do?" to help him access this state).

The person you use as your shortcut can be anyone: a person from your life, like a friend or family member; a famous person; a religious or spiritual figure; or a fictional figure from your favorite novel or movie. Who represents wise mind for you?

_____

Notice What State of Mind You're In

When you're trying to make any kind of change, you need to first increase awareness. You won't think to try to access your wise mind until you realize you're not there and you want to be. So, start checking in with yourself, at least a few times a day, to see what state of mind you're in: What part is up front right now? An emotional part, a reasoning part, or your wise mind? If you struggle to remember to do this check in, pair it with something you do multiple times daily. Every time you eat (as long as you eat at least three times a day) or every time you wash your hands, for example, you can use that as a cue to ask, "What state of mind am I in?" Sticky notes and cell phone reminders can also come in handy!

Ask Your Wise Mind a Question

It can be helpful to practice communicating with your wise mind: start checking in with this part of yourself, asking it what you should do or what it thinks about a situation you're facing. The trick here is to do this before emotions become intense: if your emotional or reasoning mind are already in charge, wise mind will be more difficult to access. You might decide to incorporate this into your daily routine as well. Every morning at breakfast, for example, you could ask your wise mind what it thinks about your plans for the day. As time goes on and with practice, you'll be more able to draw on this internal wisdom when things are more difficult.

Practice Mindfulness

Most mindfulness practices will help you access your wise mind. Remember, focusing on one thing at a time, in the present moment, with your full attention, and with acceptance typically means less emotional pain—and you may become aware that you're *not* in your wise mind at this point, which helps you move toward it! You might want to experiment with guided mindfulness practices (or you may have a practice you use already that helps you get to your wise mind).

Some people resonate with wise mind being in a certain area of their body (often the heart area, but see what feels right for you). Ask your wise mind a question and, as you mindfully focus on the area of your body where you sense that part, see if you get a response through body sensations.

Keep in mind that, if emotions are already intense, you might need to use other skills before turning to mindfulness: stick your face in cold water, do a forward bend, or do something to move you from red to yellow or yellow to green.

Wrapping Up

In this chapter, you've learned what mindfulness is, how it will be helpful, and how to practice it safely. Mindfulness increases your self-awareness and provides a foundation for many other skills, so it's important you understand it and practice what you're learning.

In this chapter, you also learned the DBT states of mind to help further your understanding of some of the parts activity you might be aware of within yourself and to increase your ability to access your wise mind. Over time and with practice, this will start to come more naturally, but remember that CPTSD makes everything more *complex*, so be patient with yourself and your parts. There are many more skills to come that will help you continue to put these pieces together.

CHAPTER SIX

Emotion Regulation Skills

In the last chapter, we looked at mindfulness—what it is, how it helps in dealing with the consequences of trauma, and how to do it. I hope you're practicing and remembering that skills like these don't usually come easily, especially when you've experienced trauma; practice is imperative as we'll be building on what you've learned so far in the coming chapters.

In this chapter, we'll start delving more deeply into emotions: first by looking at what you need to know about emotions and helping you consider your experience of these feeling states so you'll be more able to accurately name them (remember, you have to be able to name it to tame it!), and then by looking at skills to help you manage the emotions you struggle with.

What Is an Emotion?

If you grew up in an environment where your needs weren't met—you were abused, neglected, or you experienced relational wounding or trauma (such as emotionally absent or unattuned caregivers)—you likely have a complicated relationship with emotions. This is how people often learn to avoid emotions, and you may have become so adept at this that you don't know what you're feeling much of the time. So, let's start with the basics: what is an emotion?

We often refer to emotions as "feelings," but in fact, the feeling is just one aspect of an emotion. According to Linehan (1993), an emotion is a *full system response* involving thoughts, body sensations, urges (what you feel like doing), and behaviors (what you actually do).

It's also important to know that emotions serve different functions: they are messengers that provide us with information (for instance, anger arises to inform us a situation we're facing is unjust), motivate us to action (for example, to try to change the unjust situation), and communicate to others around us (through our facial expression, body language, and tone of voice, those around us will pick up on our anger without us having to tell them). From a DBT perspective, all emotions serve a purpose and are justified at times, meaning they make sense given the situation, so it's important we pay attention to them. But remember, emotions could be coming from our emotion mind (or a trauma part), so we'll want to access our wise mind to make choices about what to do with the emotion. We'll look at options for changing or reducing emotions in the next few chapters, but first, we need to become familiar with some of the basic emotions and their different components.

The following Emotion Reference Sheets (adapted from Van Dijk 2022) look at some of the more common painful emotions and their different components; you'll have an opportunity to consider your own experience of each of these emotions since everyone's experience of emotions is unique.

As you start to pay attention to your experience of emotions, you can refer to these reference sheets so that over time you'll be more able to accurately name them (or perhaps confirm that you're already able to do this). I'd suggest you read through these reference sheets now and come back to them at times when you're feeling a strong emotion. The emotions we're looking at here have been identified in infants and can therefore be described as hardwired in the human brain.

Emotions Reference Sheets

Anger

Anger's purpose: Anger arises when someone or something gets in the way of you moving toward a goal, or when you or someone you care about is being attacked, threatened, insulted, or hurt.

What anger does: Anger typically causes people to become aggressive, possibly causing them to physically or verbally attack what they see as dangerous, to make the threat go away. When the human race was evolving and there were constant threats in the environment, anger helped us survive.

Example of when anger is justified: You're recognizing the abuse you endured as a child. You're now dealing with CPTSD as a result, which has hampered your ability to reach your goals and you're angry that no one recognized what was happening and helped you; anger is justified.

Examples of anger thoughts: *This should never have happened; it's not fair. And it's not fair that I'm paying the price for the things that were done to me.* Anger thoughts often involve judgment (like *it's not fair* or *this shouldn't be happening*).

Activity: Describe Your Anger

Describe a recent time you felt angry: _____

_____

Body sensations: Look at the physical sensations connected to anger and check off any that you experienced in this situation.

☐   Tense muscles, such as clenching fists or jaw

☐   Trembling or shaking

☐   Racing heart

☐   Increased breathing rate

☐   Change in body temperature, which might lead to feeling hot or cold

☐   Other:_____

What urges did you notice? _____

_____

What did you actually do? _____

_____

Other words for anger: If *anger* doesn't quite fit how you felt in the situation you described, circle the word(s) that better describe how you felt.

Annoyed	Frustrated	Irritated	Exasperated
Resentful	Bitter	Mad	Irate
Furious	Aggravated	Bothered	Incensed
Impatient	Enraged	Outraged	Hostile
Indignant			

If you can think of other words that fit better, add them here: _____

_____

Keep in mind that just because a feeling is justified doesn't mean you should act on the urges associated with it. For example, you can feel anger at your older sibling for leaving home and not being there to protect you, and not verbally abuse them for having done so.

Fear and Anxiety

Anxiety is different from but very related to fear. They feel the same physically, but fear is present-focused and related to a specific threat, triggering the fight-or-flight response to help you survive; anxiety is future-focused and comes up when there's a more general threat you're worrying about—something that hasn't happened and may never happen. Anxiety also comes up when there's something you might reasonably expect to happen, but you expect the results to be catastrophic or out of proportion with reality. So, if you're driving on the highway and you're thinking *What if someone hits me?* you're likely going to feel anxious.

While there are times when fear is justified, there isn't really a time when you *should* feel anxious, or when you can say that anxiety is justified, because anxiety involves a fear of something that isn't a real threat—even if it feels that way! However, without some anxiety, you might take more risks, like driving dangerously. So, we're not trying to get rid of anxiety (or any emotion, since all emotions serve a purpose), but if you have anxiety regularly—or to the extreme, such as panic attacks—you want you to be able to manage it better, instead of letting it control you.

Fear's purpose: Fear is justified when there's a threat to your health, your safety, or your well-being or to that of someone you care about.

What fear does: Fear motivates you to act to protect yourself or those you care about.

Example of when fear is justified: You want to leave your abusive partner, but they've threatened to take the children and they've done this before. Fear is justified because the safety of your loved ones is threatened.

Examples of anxious thoughts: Anxious thoughts are future-focused worry thoughts often consisting of *what-ifs: What if I make a fool of myself? What if I can't do it? What if I never find someone else who loves me?*

Activity: Describe Your Anxiety

Describe a recent time you felt fearful or anxious: _____

_____

Body sensations: Look at the physical sensations connected to fear and anxiety and check off those you experienced in the situation.

- ☐ Tense or tight muscles

- ☐ Trembling or shaking muscles

- ☐ Racing heart

- ☐ Increased breathing rate

- ☐ Change in body temperature, which might lead to feeling hot or cold

- ☐ Other: _____

As you recall your experience of fear or anxiety, did you notice a similarity to what you experience when you feel angry? The body sensations can be very much the same, which is one reason why it can be easy to mix up feelings of fear or anxiety and anger!

Urges and behaviors: With fear, urges and behaviors include running away from the threat to protect yourself or others. With anxiety, urges and behaviors involve avoiding a situation (like choosing not to go to work because you're worried that you'll have a panic attack and make a fool of yourself) or escaping the situation if you're already in it (like leaving work early because you're feeling anxious).

What urges did you notice when you were in the situation you described? _____

_____

What did you actually do? _____

_____

Other words for fear: If *fear* doesn't quite fit how you felt in the situation you described, circle the word(s) that better describe how you felt.

Panicky	Terrified	Scared	Apprehensive
Nervous	Worried	Dreading	Disturbed
Stressed	Startled	Alarmed	Edgy
Jumpy	Jittery	Troubled	Anxious
Concerned	Uneasy		

If you can think of other words that fit better, add them here: _____

Sadness

Sadness's purpose: Sadness is the emotion felt when things aren't the way you expected them to be or when you've experienced a loss.

What sadness does: This is the emotion that motivates you to try to regain what you've lost, or to seek comfort from others; sadness might also encourage those around you to try to be of help or offer support.

Examples of when sadness is justified: You think about your younger self and your needs that went unmet; your partner is ending your relationship; or someone close to you is diagnosed with a terminal illness.

Examples of sad thoughts: When we're feeling sad, the tendency is to focus on the loss we've experienced and the disappointment we feel. Some examples of sad thoughts include *Things are hopeless/pointless, I'm not worthwhile,* or *I have no one.*

Activity: Describe Your Sadness

Describe a recent time you felt sadness: _____

_____

Body sensations: Look at the physical sensations connected to sadness and check off those you experienced in the situation.

- ☐ Tightness in chest or throat

- ☐ Heaviness in chest or heart

- ☐ Tears in eyes

- ☐ Slumped posture

- ☐ Tired or heavy body

- ☐ Other:_____

Urges and behaviors: Urges and behaviors associated with feeling sad often involve withdrawing from others or crying.

What urges did you notice when you were in the situation you described? _____

_____

What did you actually do? _____

_____

Other words for sadness: If *sadness* doesn't quite fit how you felt in the situation you described, circle the word(s) that better describe how you felt.

Disappointed	Discouraged	Distraught	Resigned
Hopeless	Miserable	Despair	Grief
Sorrow	Down	Distressed	Depressed
Heartbroken	Unhappy	Despondent	

If you can think of other words that fit better, add them here: _____

_____

Envy

Envy's purpose: Envy is the emotion that comes up when someone has something you want.

What envy does: Healthy envy motivates us to work to get what we want. For example, if you envy a coworker who received recognition at work, you'll work harder so you might also be rewarded. But envy can also play out in unhealthy urges, such as acting in ways to try to make the other person look bad to others, or trying to take away or ruin what they have.

Example of when envy is justified: You have feelings for your best friend's partner—you envy your best friend for that relationship. Seeing someone who seems to have everything—lots of money, a great career, a beautiful house, a happy marriage—wanting (understandably!) what that person has is justified.

Examples of envy thoughts: When envy is accompanied by feelings of happiness for the other person, it can be quite healthy. As noted earlier, envy can motivate us to work to get the things we want: *I'm happy my coworker got that promotion, but damn, I wish that had been me!* When envy is accompanied instead by feelings of anger, it can be detrimental and cause us to get stuck in self-pity and unhealthy behaviors: *It's not fair; why can't I have that? Why do they get all the luck and I get nothing but suffering in life?*

Activity: Describe Your Envy

Describe a recent time you felt envy: _____

_____

Body sensations: Look at the physical sensations connected to envy and check off those you experienced in the situation.

- ☐ Tight or rigid muscles

- ☐ Teeth clenching

- ☐ Mouth tightening

- ☐ Face flushing

- ☐ Pain in the pit of the stomach

- ☐ Other: _____

Urges and behaviors: Healthy urges and behaviors related to envy usually involve pushing yourself to try harder to improve yourself or your situation. Unhealthy urges and behaviors include attacking, criticizing, or avoiding the person you envy, or doing something to make them fail, look bad to others, or lose what they have.

What urges did you notice when you were in the situation you described? _____

_____

What did you actually do? _____

_____

Other words for envy: If *envy* doesn't quite fit how you felt in the situation you described, circle the word(s) that better describe how you felt.

Craving   Covetous   Hungry   Wanting

Desirous   Longing   Resentful

If you can think of other words that fit better, add them here: _____

_____

Jealousy

Jealousy's purpose: This emotion arises when an important relationship or sense of belonging is in danger of being lost or taken away (so, the main difference between envy and jealousy is that envy is a desire for something that others have; jealousy is a fear of losing something or someone you care about).

What jealousy does: Jealousy typically causes people to try to protect what's "theirs" (whether accurate or not!) and to not share the people or things they're afraid of losing.

Examples of when jealousy is justified: You find out your partner has been talking to their ex. Or, you reached out to two of your close friends to get together, but no one responded; weeks later you find out they met up without you—ouch.

Examples of jealous thoughts: *They're going to leave me. No one cares about me. I'm going to lose everything.* Jealousy can also be thought of as anxiety about losing someone or something that's important to you.

Activity: Describe Your Jealousy

Describe a recent time you felt jealous: _____

_____

Body sensations: Look at the physical sensations connected to jealousy and check off those you experienced in the situation.

- ☐ Racing heart

- ☐ Breathlessness

- ☐ Choking sensation

☐ Lump in throat

☐ Tense or tight muscles, such as clenching teeth

☐ Other: _____

Urges and behaviors: Urges and behaviors associated with jealousy include being violent or threatening violence toward the person you feel threatened by; trying to control the person you're afraid of losing, including interrogating or accusing them, or snooping through their belongings; acting in a clinging, dependent way; or increasing demonstrations of love, like trying to spend more time together.

What urges did you notice when you were in the situation you described? _____

_____

What did you actually do? _____

_____

Other words for jealousy: If *jealousy* doesn't quite fit how you felt in the situation you described, circle the word(s) that better describe how you felt.

Protective	Suspicious	Possessive	Covetous
Distrustful	Rivalrous	Clingy	Insecure

If you can think of other words that fit better, add them here: _____

_____

Guilt

We often feel guilt and shame in the same situations, and many aspects of these emotions are similar, which can cause us to confuse them. These emotions are very common for people with CPTSD (and are very connected to that negative self-view), and shame especially can be very powerful in keeping people dysregulated. We'll cover shame in the next reference sheet.

Guilt's purpose: Guilt is the feeling that's justified when you've done something that goes against your values, and you judge your behavior.

What guilt does: Guilt motivates you to make amends and not act a certain way in the future.

Examples of when guilt is justified: You say something to hurt your partner during an argument, or your boss overpays you and you decide to keep the money and not tell them. Your behavior doesn't match your values, so you feel guilty.

Examples of guilt thoughts: When feeling guilty, we tend to think judgmental thoughts about our behavior: *That was wrong, I shouldn't have done that. It's my fault.* We might also dwell on past behaviors when feeling guilty.

Activity: Describe Your Guilt

Describe a recent time you felt guilty: _____

_____

Body sensations: Look at the physical sensations connected to guilt and check off those you experienced in the situation.

- ☐ Feeling jittery or agitated

- ☐ Hot, flushed face

- ☐ Bowed head

- ☐ Other: _____

Urges and behaviors: When feeling guilty, you often want to make amends, such as through apologizing.

What urges did you notice when you were in the situation you described? _____

_____

What did you actually do? _____

_____

Other words for guilt. If *guilt* doesn't quite fit how you felt in the situation you described, circle the word(s) that better describe how you felt.

Remorseful   Apologetic   Regretful   Self-reproachful

Contrite   Sorry

If you can think of other words that fit better, add them here:

_____

Shame

Shame's purpose: Shame protects you by keeping you connected to others. Shame arises when you judge yourself for something you've done, or for something about yourself as a person that you fear may cause people to reject you if they knew about it.

What shame does: Shame causes you to hide—your behavior, or that characteristic of yourself—so you can remain connected to people who are important to you. Shame is also the emotion that stops you from doing that behavior again in the future. If people know about your behavior (or characteristic), shame causes you to try to make amends in those relationships.

Examples of when shame is justified: You engage in a target behavior (like drinking, using drugs, or gambling) as a way of coping with your emotions and you hide the behavior so others won't reject you. Whether or not shame is justified in this example depends on who you're hiding from. Some people might reject you for what you did, in which case shame is justified; it protects you, causing you to hide the behavior and keep you connected. But others (like your significant other or your therapist) hopefully would not reject you, in which case shame isn't justified.

You may also experience shame if there's something that makes you different from others, or at least you believe it makes you different. This could include things like your trauma history, sexual or gender identity, a mental health or addiction problem, or a particular belief you hold. Hiding that part of yourself protects you from being rejected by others. It's sometimes difficult to tell if shame is justified or not because this involves knowing what others would think if they knew about this thing. For instance, many people still attach stigma to mental illness, and if your friend has previously insisted that "people shouldn't let their past hold them back," then you'll likely keep quiet about your CPTSD to avoid their judgment. Or, if your friend has confided in you about their own difficult past or mental health problems, you'll be more certain you can open up without fear of rejection.

More often than not, shame isn't justified. It often comes up, though, because it's the awful, soul-sucking feeling that arises when we judge ourselves. So, instead of thinking *I shouldn't have had that drink* (causing guilt), you're thinking *What's wrong with me that I drink to cope?* or *I'm awful.* Judging yourself for something you've done or for something you think makes you defective will cause you to feel shame.

One reason we often confuse guilt and shame is that we often feel both at the same time, as we judge our behavior (leading to guilt) and we judge ourselves for having done that behavior (leading to shame).

Examples of shame thoughts: When we feel shame, we're usually judging ourselves in some way: *I'm defective. There's something wrong with me. If others knew the real me, they would leave.* With shame, there is also often an element of fearing that others will reject us.

Activity: Describe Your Shame

Describe a recent time you felt shame: _____

_____

Body sensations: Look at the physical sensations connected to shame and check off those you experienced in the situation.

☐ Pain in the pit of the stomach

☐ Slumped posture, bowed head

☐ Hot, flushed face

☐ Sense of dread

☐ Difficulty making eye contact

☐ Other: _____

Urges and behaviors: Shame makes you want to crawl under the nearest rock and hide and isolate yourself from others, and makes eye contact with others difficult. Taken to the extreme, it can cause suicidal thoughts and behaviors.

What urges did you notice when you were in the situation you described?

_____

What did you actually do?

_____

Other words for shame: If *shame* doesn't quite fit how you felt in the situation you described, circle the word(s) that better describe how you felt.

Mortification   Self-loathing   Self-disgust

If you can think of other words that fit better, add them here: _____

_____

There aren't really many other words for shame. Sometimes we use "embarrassed" or "humiliated" to describe the emotion, but both are different from shame. Think of "embarrassed" as the feeling we have when we trip up the stairs or walk out of the bathroom with TP stuck to our foot: when we're embarrassed, we can laugh at ourselves or the situation later. "Humiliation" is a little closer to shame, but also involves anger—the sense of someone having caused us to feel shame when we didn't deserve it. In this sense, humiliation is usually more tolerable than shame because anger often drives us to talk to others and seek validation for our feelings; shame keeps us disconnected and hiding.

This list might not include all the emotions you find difficult to bear, but they are the more commonly distressing ones. This knowledge is just the beginning, however; what's even more important is that you're considering how this information applies to you, and how you can use it in your life. We're not usually explicitly taught about emotions when we're growing up; instead, we assume we know what we feel rather than exploring this further.

Let's get you applying what you're learning by thinking about situations in your own life with the following Awareness of Emotions Worksheet (from Van Dijk 2022). Fill out one of these worksheets when you have an emotion; my recommendation would be at least a couple of times each week to increase your familiarity with your emotions. It's usually most helpful to complete the worksheet as soon after the emotionally charged situation as possible. I've included a sample worksheet for your reference, as well as a blank worksheet, which you can also download at this book's website: http://www.newharbinger.com/53103.

Awareness of Emotions Worksheet: Example

Description of the situation that triggered the emotion (just the facts!): My supervisor, Tamara, was off sick. Our secretary called asking me to assist a client who had come in for an appointment with her, not having received the message that she was away. I spoke to the client and was able to help; they left satisfied. On Tamara's return to the office, she reprimanded me for intervening with her client and asked me not to do this again.

What thoughts did you have about this situation (including judgments, interpretations, assumptions)? What's wrong with her?! I did her a favor by helping; I didn't get anything out of it, but she's worried I'll make her look bad. I know she just wants me gone.

What physical sensations did you notice? Heat in my body, heart racing, shallow breath, shaking, muscle tension.

What urges did you experience? I wanted to yell at Tamara and tell her how selfish she is.

What did you actually do? I didn't say anything. I hid in my office because I don't want her to see how much this bothers me. I also don't want to rock the boat at work because I know she's doing her best to get rid of me.

What is the name of the emotion(s) you were experiencing? Anger and anxiety.

Awareness of Emotions Worksheet

Description of the situation that triggered the emotion (just the facts!): _____

_____

_____

_____

_____

What thoughts did you have about this situation (including judgments, interpretations, assumptions)?

_____

_____

_____

What physical sensations did you notice? _____

_____

What urges did you experience? _____

_____

What did you actually do? _____

_____

_____

What is the name of the emotion(s) you were experiencing? _____

_____

Mindfulness of Emotions

You may be struggling to notice things you're being asked to notice in this chapter—many people have learned that it's safer or more comfortable to avoid turning inward and paying attention to these things; it becomes second nature to ignore internal experiences instead. But hopefully, you're starting to see the importance to your recovery of increasing your self-awareness. So, how do you start to consciously access what you've pushed away for so long? One way is through mindfulness.

In chapter five, we discussed how mindfulness contributes to self-awareness, including helping us become more in tune with our emotions. The following mindfulness practice (adapted from Van Dijk 2022) will help you turn inward and pay attention, with acceptance, to those internal experiences.

Activity: Mindfulness of Emotions

To prepare for this practice, you might want to read the following script to yourself until it comes more naturally for you when you start to practice. Alternatively, you could record yourself reading the script so you can play it back to guide you through the practice until you get the hang of it. Or you could have someone read it out loud to you. You can make this practice as short or as long as you'd like, so remember to do what works best for you right now. Also remember to keep your eyes open during the practice, unless you know you won't dissociate or have flashbacks.

Start by getting as comfortable as possible, sitting in a dignified posture with your back fairly straight in your chair and feet flat on the floor. (If you experience physical pain, do your best to adopt a posture that you'll be able to stay in for the duration of the practice). Breathe deeply, noticing the feel of your belly expanding as you inhale and deflating as you exhale. When you're ready, slowly scan through your body from the top of your head all the way down to the tips of your toes, noticing any places you're holding tension. Our body often provides helpful clues for us; it's not uncommon to clench your jaw or literally sit on the edge of your seat when feeling a difficult emotion, so just observe whatever's happening in your body in this moment.

Allow yourself to become aware of any emotions that are present within you right now. (If you don't notice anything immediately, continue to scan through your body until you pick up on something, however small or neutral it may seem.) Where do you feel the emotion most strongly? Be curious about the sensations you notice as best as you can, exploring them with openness. It's natural to want to avoid or resist emotions and sensations, especially if they're uncomfortable, but see if you can be curious about them instead, just for a moment. Remember to breathe.

Now see if you can nonjudgmentally label your experience: factually describe what you notice in your body. For instance, you might come up with a word to describe the sensation of the feeling, such as *tight*, *butterflies*, *knot*, or *hard*. Notice the size of the feeling: does it feel small, medium, or large? Perhaps it seems to have a temperature: *hot*, *cold*, or somewhere in between. Go with whatever feels right; you're just listening to your body, noticing any sensations and the emotions they might reveal. You're not trying to make anything happen nor are you trying to stop anything from happening.

If you can, put a label on the emotion, such as *bored*, *anxious*, or *content*. If you can't put a name on it, just notice that. If you notice a thought or a story that's related to the emotion, just notice it without judging, as best as you can, and bring your attention back to whatever physical sensations are most prominent right now.

If an emotion feels uncomfortable or distressing, see if you can breathe into it, continue to observe it, and remind yourself that it isn't permanent: emotions come and go. If it gets to be too much, you can stop the practice and come back to it another time.

Over time, this practice will help you recognize the different components of your emotions so that you'll be more able to accurately label them. For now, let's get you thinking about the practice you just did by answering the following questions.

What did you notice in your body? _____

_____

_____

What did you notice about your thoughts? _____

_____

_____

What did you notice about your emotions? _____

_____

_____

Were you able to distinguish between the physical, mental, and emotional parts of your experience?

_____

_____

Did you notice the emotions change in any way? _____

_____

_____

Did you notice any thoughts that brought up or intensified an emotion or physical sensation?

_____

_____

It makes sense that this exercise might be painful, which is another reason to keep the practice short to start; you'll likely find your ability to tolerate will grow as you practice. But if this exercise didn't resonate for you, or if you found it too difficult, know that there will be other tips to work on this as we go; you'll also learn other skills to decrease the intensity of emotions—starting with the next DBT skill of *nonjudgmental stance* (Linehan 2014).

Taking a Nonjudgmental Stance

For many of us, judgments are part of life: we judge ourselves, others, and situations; and we hear others judging regularly, which normalizes this behavior—so much so that it becomes something we don't question, and we don't consider the effects these judgments might be having on us. For those who've grown up in abusive or pervasively invalidating environments, this tends to be even more of a problem, often leading to chronic shame and other intensely painful emotions.

Taking a nonjudgmental stance is about becoming aware of the language you're using, so you have the option of reducing judgments to decrease emotional pain. Let's start by looking at what we mean by *judgment*.

What Is a Judgment?

In this context, a judgment is a word we don't typically use in a neutral way that provides a short-form, nonfactual label for someone or something. Examples include, *I'm worthless*; *They're an idiot*; *That was bad*. Hopefully, you can see that these judgments—*worthless, idiot, bad*—aren't words we use in a neutral way; they aren't facts. A *fact*, by the way, is something that is *known to be true*. It is a fact that 2 + 2 = 4. It is a fact the sun rises and sets every single day and one year consists of 365 days. Judgments are not facts (no, it is not a fact someone is an idiot!). Judgments also don't provide us with information—if I told you that someone was being an idiot, you'd have no idea what I meant by that since the word *idiot* will mean different things to different people and different people will evaluate behavior in different ways (you might not see anything problematic with that person's behavior).

Why does this matter? Judgments often inflame our emotions—in fact, another way of thinking of judgments is *inflammatory language*. Judgments add fuel to our emotional fire. So, what might start as irritation that your partner forgot to take the garbage out, for example, can escalate to anger when you're judging them as an idiot for forgetting! To be clear, being nonjudgmental doesn't typically eliminate an emotion but it helps prevent extra emotions from arising. Let's also be clear that I'm not suggesting you try to eradicate judgments—that's impossible, and not necessary. But becoming aware of when judgments are inflaming your emotions allows you the choice of doing something about them to prevent extra emotional pain.

What to Do with Judgments

Once you've become aware of your judgments, you have three options: First, you might choose to continue judging. Let's be honest, it can feel satisfying to let those judgments fly! But are they helpful? That's the question you need to ask yourself. When you're aware that they're not—and potentially even causing harm—hopefully, you'll consider the other options. The second option is to let it go. Just stop judging. This tends to be more doable when we're not emotionally attached to what we're judging, such as *I think it's weird when people dye their hair green*. It doesn't impact my life if people dye their hair green, so I can easily accept that some people do this. Not so easy, however, when we're more emotionally invested (for instance, if the person dying their hair green is my child). So, what then? Option three: we change the judgment to a *nonjudgmental* (or neutral) statement.

I've come to define a nonjudgmental statement as consisting of two things: the facts of the situation (from our perspective, of course) and our emotions. Returning to my earlier example, a nonjudgmental statement might be, *I'm irritated with my partner for forgetting to put the garbage out.* My irritation is not likely going to disappear because I stop judging my partner but I'm not inflaming the emotion, which means my irritation is likely to stay just that, rather than turning into something more.

Activity: Taking a Nonjudgmental Stance

Now it's your turn to practice. Read the following scenarios and follow the steps to create a nonjudgmental statement. You can read suggestions for nonjudgmental statements at the end of the chapter. The first one has been completed as an example for you to follow.

1. Cari judges himself as *worthless* for having been unfaithful to his partner many years ago.

    What's the judgment we're eliminating? I'm worthless.

    What are the facts of the situation? I cheated on my partner.

    What emotion(s) do you think Cari might be feeling? Shame.

    Nonjudgmental statement combining facts and emotions: I feel shame for cheating on my partner.

2. Felicia judges her friends as immature because they like to party every weekend and continue to live their lives as though they're in high school, even though they're now thirty. She feels like she doesn't fit in with them because their values are so different.

    What's the judgment we're eliminating?

    _____

    What are the facts of the situation? _____

    _____

    _____

    _____

What emotion(s) do you think Felicia might be feeling?

_____

Nonjudgmental statement combining facts and emotions: _____

_____

_____

3.   Niall's parents physically abused and neglected him and his siblings when they were growing up and now he judges them as terrible parents.

What's the judgment we're eliminating?

_____

What are the facts of the situation? _____

_____

_____

_____

What emotion(s) do you think Niall might be feeling?

_____

Nonjudgmental statement combining facts and emotions: _____

_____

_____

Now it's your turn to think of your own judgments and go through this same exercise. If you need help, consider asking someone you're comfortable with. You might also start with some of the less complicated judgments you find yourself making, such as judging other people's driving, or when your favorite sports team is losing.

Describe the situation in which you're judging: _____

_____

_____

What's the judgment we're eliminating? _____

_____

What are the facts of the situation? _____

_____

_____

What are the emotions you're feeling?

_____

Nonjudgmental statement combining facts and emotions: _____

_____

_____

Describe the situation in which you're judging: _____

_____

_____

What's the judgment we're eliminating? _____

_____

What are the facts of the situation? _____

_____

_____

What are the emotions you're feeling?

_____

Nonjudgmental statement combining facts and emotions: _____

_____

_____

This is a complicated skill, so practice is key; over time, being nonjudgmental will start to come more naturally. Just remember that you get to choose when you want to practice being nonjudgmental (or any skill); also remember that the more you use this new way of thinking, the more you'll be able to reduce your emotional pain.

The Challenge of Self-Judgments

I mentioned earlier that shame is a common emotion for people with CPTSD (often related to that negative self-view). If this is the case for you, I'd encourage you to do some practice with judgments of others or situations until you get more comfortable with this skill, then you can target your self-judgments more directly. Let's revisit the example with Cari to help you see how you might do this.

Cari often judges himself as a *bad* partner. To work on changing this negative self-view, he considers why he judges himself in this way:

- I was unfaithful to my partner.

- I get jealous and sometimes check my partner's phone without telling them.

- I lash out at my partner when I'm angry.

By writing out this list, Cari has completed step one of creating a nonjudgmental statement: he's now got the facts of the situations in which he judges himself to be a bad partner; now he just needs to add the emotions and he has a list of nonjudgmental statements. The emotions might be different in each of these scenarios, or Cari might find that the emotion is the same (for instance, shame). Remember, the emotion won't necessarily disappear altogether, but when Cari is less judgmental toward himself, he stops inflaming his emotions, making them more manageable; in the long run, his self-compassion will likely increase.

Let's look now at a way of being nonjudgmental with your emotions that will help you manage them more effectively: *self-validation*.

Self-Invalidation

An abusive, neglectful, or otherwise pervasively invalidating environment typically teaches people to *in*validate themselves—to not accept, trust, or even acknowledge their internal experiences (such as emotions, thoughts, and physical sensations). This can show up in many ways even when you're no longer living in that environment: I often see people with complex trauma neglect their body by not eating properly or not drinking enough fluids. This may be related to being out of touch with body sensations, with no awareness of feelings of hunger or thirst; even when there is awareness, there's often a tendency to disregard those sensations. There's often a tendency to put their own needs last, prioritizing everyone else and not engaging in self-care. The message to self here is *My needs/wants* *don't matter.* Emotional self-invalidation is also quite common: ignoring, avoiding, judging, or otherwise pushing emotions away (consciously or unconsciously).

While all of these are important for you to consider in relation to your own experience, we're going to focus on emotional self-invalidation.

What Is Self-Invalidation?

Invalidating your emotion means you're judging your emotion in some way, whether with words (for instance, *This is stupid; I shouldn't be feeling this way*) or through not being willing to have the experience and trying to get rid of it (often through a target behavior).

It's understandable that if something's uncomfortable, we don't want to experience it, but invalidating ourselves typically increases emotional pain. Let's look at Marjana as an example.

Marjana's Story

Marjana grew up in a family that couldn't tolerate displays of intense emotion. Whether she was angry at her siblings, afraid of the dark, or excited about some good news she'd received, the message was the same: calm down, you're being too emotional, too loud, too much. She was often sent to her room because of her inability to control her emotions and this left her feeling disconnected from her family, like she didn't fit in, and ashamed. The result was Marjana doing her best to avoid feeling those emotions and this pattern has continued for her as an adult. She often successfully squashes the emotion before it can intensify, but when she's in the car by herself, especially driving home from work after a hard day, anger will often emerge—at the person who doesn't signal to change lanes, or someone who squeezes in front of her at the last minute—and she's quickly enraged. When she finally catches herself, the judgments turn inward: What's wrong with me that I get so angry? I'm an awful person, and so on. Now, not only does Marjana feel angry at the person or situation that caused the anger in the first place but she also feels guilt, shame, and anger at herself for feeling angry.

The Consequences of Invalidating Our Emotions

Since we're judging ourselves for the feeling, invalidation also inflames our emotions. Let's break this down using Marjana's example so you can see why.

First, Marjana encounters a situation that causes her to feel angry. This is what we refer to as a *primary emotion*—the first emotion that arises, or the *first responder* when we encounter a stimulus (just to complicate matters, there can be more than one primary emotion). If Marjana validated her primary emotion (anger), she would likely only experience that emotion; instead, she judges herself for it, and this leads to *secondary emotions*—how we feel about our feelings (Linehan 2014). In this example, Marjana feels guilt, shame, and anger at herself for feeling angry. It's not uncommon to experience more than one secondary emotion when we invalidate ourselves. But here's the moral of this story: if we don't judge ourselves for feeling the primary emotion—if we validate it instead—then no secondary emotions will be triggered.

Ways of Validating Emotions

Following are the three ways of self-validating that I teach my clients (Van Dijk 2012):

1. *Acknowledging:* The first and simplest way of self-validating is acknowledging the presence of the emotion: "I feel angry." By just naming the emotion (as long as you name it accurately), you're validating it. (Tip: if you're not yet able to name your emotions accurately, I'd suggest you return to doing the work in chapter six; while you work on this, however, you can self-validate through using a generic statement like, *I don't know what I'm feeling right now, but whatever it is, it's okay that I feel it*).

2. *Allowing:* The second way of self-validating is giving yourself permission to feel the emotion: "It's okay that I feel angry." Not only are you not judging the emotion but you're also going one step further and saying, *This is okay*—not meaning that you like it, but that you're allowed to feel it.

3. *Understanding:* This way of validating oneself is typically the most difficult because you're indicating an understanding of the emotion given the current situation or based on your past. For instance, "It makes sense that I feel angry because that person just cut me off" (present context), or "It makes sense that I get angry when I'm driving because this is what I learned from my mom" (historical context).

Keep in mind that we don't always understand why we're feeling a certain way, so we won't always be able to validate our emotion like this. If that's the case, we can still validate it by either acknowledging it or allowing it. And the bottom line is that, as long as we're not *in*validating the emotion, we're not generating secondary emotions.

Activity: What Emotions Do You Need to Validate?

1. In this activity, you'll have an opportunity to consider how you do when it comes to validating your emotions and some ways to improve in this area. What emotions do you struggle to accept in yourself? Circle the ones you struggle with.

    Anger   Guilt   Shame   Fear

    Jealousy   Envy   Sadness   Happiness

    Other: _____   Other: _____

2. Choose one of the emotions you circled in question #1 that you'll start to work on validating (remember, doing one at a time typically works best—if you circled more than one, you can come back to work on the others later). Write the emotion you'll start with here:

    _____

3. Write some of your thoughts about this emotion: Does it mean something about you as a person if you feel this way? Do you know where these beliefs developed? (Keep in mind messages about emotions commonly come from our family of origin, as well as from our community, and messages can be overt where we're verbally told we *shouldn't* feel a certain emotion, or more covert, where we learn in more subtle ways that we shouldn't feel certain emotions.) Write your thoughts here:

    _____

    _____

    _____

4. Thinking of the three ways of validating that you've just learned, how can you talk back to these thoughts when you feel this emotion? Write some validating statements for yourself here:

_____

_____

_____

Now, of course, the important thing is to practice changing the way you talk to yourself about this emotion. When you notice the emotion arising, read your validating statements to yourself to help change your self-talk. You can also read these statements to yourself more proactively—just for the sake of practicing them, pull out your list and review it now and then. The more you review these validating statements, the more naturally they'll come, even when the feeling arises.

Wrapping Up

You've learned a lot about emotions in this chapter, and hopefully, you're using the reference sheets and the worksheet provided to increase (or evaluate) your ability to name emotions accurately. You also had the opportunity to do a mindfulness practice to help with this and you learned the skills of nonjudgmental stance and self-validation to help you manage those painful emotions by not adding more fuel to your emotional fire.

Remember to take good care of yourself as you work through this book, going at a pace that feels right for you, even if that means temporarily putting it aside so you can work on putting into practice what you're learning or skipping some sections that might be too triggering for you right now. Remember, we're still in stage one at this point, with the goal being stabilization, although some of these skills will also be very helpful in stage three.

In the next chapter, we're going to dip our toes into stage two, deepening your understanding of your self-system (your parts) and giving you some strategies to work with these different aspects of yourself. If you don't feel ready for this just yet, feel free to pause and continue practicing what you've learned so far, or to move on to chapter eight, where we'll be getting into more stage three skills to help you move on from your trauma and build a life worth living.

Answers to Nonjudgmental Stance Activity

What's the judgment we're eliminating? *They're immature.*

Facts: *My friends and I now have very different values and I don't seem to fit in with them anymore because I'm moving on and growing up and they're still partying like they're twenty.*

Emotions: *Annoyed and disappointed in them.*

Nonjudgmental statement: *I don't feel like I fit in with my friends anymore, I don't like the way they're acting, and I feel annoyed and disappointed in them for not wanting the same things I do.*

What's the judgment we're eliminating? *Mom and Dad were terrible parents.*

Facts: *Mom and Dad used to hit us and would make us fend for ourselves to get meals, do our own laundry, and so on from a very young age.*

Emotions: *Angry and sad.*

Nonjudgmental statement: *It makes me angry and sad to think of how our parents treated us.*

CHAPTER SEVEN

Coming to Terms with Trauma

So far in this workbook, we've been focusing on stage one, where you've been learning about the effects of trauma and skills to increase safety and stability in your life. In this chapter, we'll be delving more into working with your parts. This may still be about stabilization if you have a particularly complicated self-system; but this may also be stage two work, where you're working on resolving past traumas. Just to be clear, the trauma resolution work of stage two isn't necessarily about remembering the traumas you've experienced but about finding ways to acknowledge what happened without reliving it.

In this chapter, you'll have the chance to become more familiar with your parts and learn to communicate with them more effectively. You'll also learn skills to orient your parts, helping them move out of the past and into the present, thereby reducing reexperiencing and helping your system come to terms with the trauma you've experienced. Finally, we'll look at a DBT skill to help you come to terms with your trauma through acknowledging reality.

A note before we start: you're likely learning a lot about yourself as you do this work, and while self-awareness is crucial, it can also be painful. If at any point you feel you need a break, please take it. You might also need to go back to review skills to maintain your stability as you do this work. And if you feel you need support, please be sure to reach out to a healthcare professional or someone in your support network.

What Are Parts?

First, if you're struggling with the idea of having "parts," you're not alone! When I started learning about this, I thought it was weird, even though I sometimes used that language myself—"Part of me wants to do this, and part of me knows that's not a wise choice." Then I began to see parts as the states of mind from DBT: I could certainly relate to having an emotional, reasoning, and wise part.

Sometimes, finding the language that fits best for you can help, so here are some other ways to conceptualize parts:

- Parts are memory networks: they include information related to a specific time in your life or a certain event, so you may have parts related to specific experiences you've had (for instance, you might have a part that gets anxious when you drive after having a car accident).

- Fisher describes young parts as "the child you once were at a certain age or the child you had to be in certain situations. It's the little you" (Fisher 2017, 155). Therefore, you might notice parts as yourself at different ages: your three-year-old part, your sixteen-year-old part, and so on.

- As you learned in chapter two, parts can be based on defense systems, so you might identify fight, flight, freeze, submit, or attach parts.

These different parts or aspects of self we all have are also known as *ego states*, defined as an "organized system of behavior and experience…bound together by some common principles, and… separated from other such states by a boundary that is more or less permeable" (Watkins and Watkins 1997, 25).

Ego states occur on a continuum. On one end of the spectrum, there are the healthy, adaptive parts; they have permeable boundaries, allowing awareness of other parts and the information each holds. For example, I remember my father once commenting, "That's not you!" after hearing me speak professionally—apparently, he had never met my therapist part. Think of an area of your own life where you bring a specific set of skills or mindset. For instance, if you're a parent, you likely act differently when you're playing with your children than when you're socializing with friends. Or if you're a student, sitting in class listening to the professor will involve a different part of you than sitting in a theater watching a movie. But you have awareness of these other parts of yourself and access to the memories and knowledge they hold.

At the opposite end of the spectrum, we see extreme separation of parts (as in DID); they have rigid, impermeable boundaries, preventing awareness of other parts and blocking access to the information held by one another.

In the middle of this ego-state continuum, the boundaries are more permeable, but there is still an unhealthy separation of parts. If you have CPTSD, you'll likely have less conscious awareness of your parts, less ability to communicate with them, and more internal conflict. In this scenario, you'll be more likely to have experiences of not understanding yourself and your emotional reactions, for example.

Ego states can develop in three ways (Watkins and Watkins 1997):

1. Through normative, healthy differentiation (for example, as I learned and trained to be a psychotherapist, I developed my therapist part).

2. By unconsciously internalizing certain qualities of others, such as beliefs, values, and behaviors. This commonly happens with children and parents. For example, if your parents always ensured you said please and thank you as a child, as an adult, you may judge people who don't say please and thank you as impolite. Your parents' value has been internalized as your own.

3. As a reaction to trauma: Experiencing traumatic events can lead to the formation of parts associated with those events. For instance, a child who is verbally and emotionally abused by a male caregiver develops a part that's triggered when they interact with male authority figures. When a trauma part is activated, you may reexperience emotions, thoughts, and physical sensations associated with the original trauma.

Hopefully this idea of parts—and the fact that everyone has them, to varying degrees—is starting to resonate for you. You may have already started to develop an awareness of some of your parts, but since awareness is the first step to making changes, I'm going to help you learn more about your internal system.

Getting to Know Your Parts

As you begin learning about your internal system, you may find that there are certain parts you struggle with—you might not like some parts, or you may feel anger, fear, shame, or other painful emotions toward them. It's important for you to know that parts are trying to protect you, even if that's not readily apparent. You might recall Cory from chapter two, who had thoughts of suicide related to feeling out of control; it might be difficult to see how thoughts of suicide can be protective, but from the perspective of Cory's twelve-year-old part who had no other means of feeling in control when facing his highly critical father, this becomes more understandable.

Thinking about our defense systems can also help: this may have been Cory's *fight* part, who, since he couldn't fight his father, would fantasize about fighting back differently—by doing violence to himself. Similarly, someone who turns to substances or disordered eating might be driven by a flight part trying to protect the system by escaping through these behaviors.

If you've experienced ongoing trauma, you might also develop a part that imitates your abuser; this, too, would be a protective part, keeping you safe by verbally abusing you to keep you in line so you don't incur the wrath of the abusive caregiver. The problem is that this part isn't aware the abuse is over and their means of protecting you is now harmful.

It's important to bear in mind that we're not trying to get rid of parts! The goal of this work is to help you develop healthy communication and cooperation between you and your parts so your whole system is working together to accomplish the same goals. All parts play an important role, so we want them to continue to do their jobs, but in a way that's more effective and will make everyone's jobs easier! This is also where mindfulness will be helpful: as you notice an internal experience, as best as you can, just allow yourself to be aware of it and nonjudgmentally describe it. Mindful observation like this activates the prefrontal cortex—simply put, the thinking part of your brain—which will help you put a little distance between you and the experience, making it more likely you'll be able to act from your wise mind. You'll see this in action when we talk about unblending later in this chapter.

In the following activity (based on Fraser 1991), you'll have an opportunity to meet and dialogue with your parts. I might sound like a broken record, but remember that stability must come first, so please check in with yourself as you do this activity and go at a pace that feels right for you, even if that means stopping if things become too painful—you can always come back to this another time.

As you get to know your parts over time, you'll want to have a way of referring to them. Please be sure to use nonjudgmental language: even if you have complex emotions toward certain parts, it's important to be respectful. For instance, I had a client who had a part she initially referred to as "The Reject"—ouch! After some discussion, she renamed this part "The Rejected Part," indicating that this is how the part felt, rejected by others.

One more thing before we move into this exercise: for some people, this exercise will feel like a natural experience—you might already have conversations with your parts (essentially, this is just a more elaborate form of talking to yourself). For others, however, it might feel strange, weird, or you might find yourself (or part of you) judging it as stupid. Trust me, I get it! But let me remind you that we all have parts. I myself have been surprised at times to see how helpful this is for my clients (with and without CPTSD), so I'm asking that you do your best to be open to this experiment.

Activity: Meeting Your Parts

To begin this activity, be sure you have some time where you can sit quietly, without interruption. If you're feeling unsure about whether you're ready to meet your parts, consider having a support person close by if that's comfortable or possible. I'd also suggest setting a timer for this activity, starting with five minutes, in case you dissociate. Most people find it helps to close their eyes for this activity, but do what feels wise for you. This activity usually involves visualizing, but if you struggle to do so (or if you know dissociation is possible), you can draw your meeting place and parts as they come in (don't worry if you're not an artist!).

Start by imagining a neutral space where you'll meet with your parts (this is a different space from your calm place, from chapter four). This can be a real or imagined place; it can be an indoor or outdoor space, but you'll want it to be comfortable for all parts and not associated with traumas. You can decorate this place however you'd like, bringing in chairs, couches, blankets, pillows, or whatever you'd like to make it comfortable. Of course, since this is your imagination, you can also make changes as you go. Let yourself settle in for a few moments until you have a good sense of the space—if possible, notice what you see, feel, hear, and smell. Finally, you'll want to create a door to this space if there isn't one already—if your meeting place is outside, for example, you might create a fence with a gate or a magic door that leads to that space.

When you're ready, open the door and invite in any parts that would like to join you. All parts are welcome, but this is strictly voluntary, so parts get to choose to come or not. Some parts might just observe without participating; others may want to stay outside the meeting place and watch from a distance. Allow parts to be wherever's most comfortable for them.

Parts may look like other versions of yourself (for instance, you at different ages), but they might also take different forms: you may have parts that identify as a gender different from yours, that appear as animals, or even inanimate objects. Sometimes parts are insubstantial, like smoke or mist, or you might get more of a felt sense of their presence, rather than seeing them; communications from parts may be in the form of emotions or body sensations. Just allow yourself to observe whatever happens. If no parts come at all, that's okay—just remain in the meeting place for a while if that's comfortable and get used to being in that space.

If you do have parts that come in, the next step is ensuring safety. Send your parts the following message with your words and your body: This is a safe place for everyone, where we're working on getting to know one another; therefore, everyone must agree not to hurt anyone else (including you!). If you have a part who refuses to abide by this rule (You might actually hear voices in your head—no you're not *crazy*. This might present as thoughts of self-harm or suicide; or just thoughts about how stupid this exercise is and that there's no way you're going to do this), please turn to the section where I'll discuss how to close the meeting place. If parts are agreeable (which you might experience as curiosity, interest, and calm), continue with the exercise.

Thank your parts for joining you, and if you'd like, ask if anyone has questions or comments. There's no specific agenda for this first visit, other than beginning to get to know parts. You might have a short dialogue with parts or, if no one has anything to say, you can move on to closing the meeting place.

Closing the Meeting Place

When you're ready to finish the exercise, thank your parts for coming (even if they didn't agree to safety and you're closing the meeting place early). Treat your parts as you would want to be treated and remember that all parts are welcome and have a role in your self-system. Let them know you'll be back again to meet with them, as you'll return to your meeting place regularly to get to know your parts and work on increasing communication and cooperation within your system.

Then, show your parts to the door and ask them to return to where they came from (if you had child parts come in, be sure that they have someone to care for them). When everyone's gone, take a good look around to make sure you haven't missed anyone—close the door, lock it up, and turn out the lights (or whatever you need to do to close your meeting place). After this practice, it's often helpful to take a trip to your calm place (from chapter four) or do something else that's calming or relaxing.

You can answer the following questions as you reflect on what this experience was like. Start by making a list or diagram of the parts who came to the meeting place (I'd suggest you keep a separate list of your parts as this document will change as you get to know your system). For each part, answer the following questions:

1. Describe the part: If you can see them, what do they look like? If you can't see them, describe your sense or experience of them:

    _____

    _____

2. How do you feel toward this part (remember to stay nonjudgmental, just noting emotions)?

    _____

    _____

3. Does this part have any emotions toward you or toward other parts? For example, it's common for parts to dislike or feel anger toward young parts because they often hold trauma material. If you have a part that imitates an abuser, other parts might fear them; if you have a freeze or attach part, other parts might be ashamed of behaviors the part engages in, such as self-harming or people-pleasing. Noticing where parts position themselves in relation to one another in the meeting place can also provide helpful information. Write what you noticed here:

_____

_____

_____

_____

If you struggle to recall anything about what happened in the meeting place, this could be related to dissociation—a sign that you're not ready for this work just yet. Please don't be discouraged! Remember the number one priority is getting and keeping you stable; not everyone will be ready to do parts work right away, so it's important to listen to what your system is telling you (there's likely a part protecting you!) and slow the work down when necessary or find a therapist who can help you do this work safely.

How often you meet with your parts will depend. It's possible (even likely) that this was uncomfortable—your parts came to be for a reason, and learning about them means potentially learning things about yourself and your past. If you struggle to function for days after doing this exercise, I again urge you to slow down and find a therapist if you're able to. If, on the other hand, you're able to bounce back—maybe you need a nap afterward (this can be exhausting work!), or you need to do a lot of self-care for the rest of the day (not a bad idea!), but then you feel like your usual self once again—going to your meeting place several days a week will be very helpful.

There will often be a specific reason for communicating with parts—perhaps you want to find out what your parts know about a certain problem or emotion, or you're struggling to make an important decision. When you open the meeting place, you'll invite in any parts that have information about that situation, as well as any parts that would like to be part of the conversation (we don't want anyone feeling left out!). But the meeting place is also a time to check in with your parts to see if they have concerns they'd like to address. Over time, you might think of this as a family meeting where your system (your "internal family") learns to work together and resolve conflicts. Let's return to Marguerite's story to see how she used the meeting place to learn about what was interfering with sleep.

Marguerite's Meeting Place

Marguerite was struggling with falling asleep at night; no matter how tired she was, as soon as she got into bed, she felt wide awake again. She had tried sleep meds prescribed by her doctor, but this didn't help. Going to her meeting place, Marguerite asked if any parts had information about the sleep problems; not surprisingly, several young parts were able to express their fear of going to bed because bedtime was often when bad things would happen. Based on the young parts' fear, Marguerite came up with a plan to help her young parts feel safer: she reminded them that they were safe with her and that they no longer lived in the family home where the bad things had happened and she would envision herself tucking them into bed with her.

But Marguerite also found out through her meeting place that she had a teenage part that just didn't want to go to bed so early! This part wanted to stay up watching her favorite show or reading. Marguerite was able to negotiate with this part so that on weekends she'd be able to stay up a little later doing things she enjoyed, but during the week, she'd get to bed at a reasonable time so she could get up more easily in the morning.

Of course, going to the meeting place is just the first step in the process of improving communication and cooperation within your self-system. Let's look at what comes next.

Working with Your Parts

Once you've started identifying and learning about your parts, you'll need to watch for parts activity, noticing when they're taking over. Hopefully, you've already been working toward this through noticing when you're in emotion or reasoning mind; mindfulness will also help, increasing awareness of emotions, thoughts, and physical sensations that will alert you to parts becoming activated. Once you become aware of this, you'll be able to act from your wise mind to *unblend* from parts.

Blending with Parts

When a part takes over and is in the driver's seat—controlling your thoughts, emotions, physical sensations, and body functions—you've become *blended* with that part (Schwartz 1995); you can't tell the difference between your experience and that of the part. This is what happens when you've been triggered, but blending with a part isn't inherently "bad"—it can be helpful when a part takes over to navigate a specific situation where that part's skills are required. Think of a parent who's a doctor—isn't it better for the doctor part to take over when their child is injured, to deal with the immediate crisis, rather than having the worried parent part in charge? But in a healthy system, the part will unblend, stepping aside for the wise self to take the wheel again once that need is resolved (in this example, when the medical crisis is over). When this doesn't happen naturally and fluidly, however—as is often the case for individuals with CPTSD when parts blend unnecessarily or stay blended—it becomes problematic.

How to Unblend

Remember that reasoning mind and emotion mind are parts, so mindfully noticing when you're acting from one of these states and using skills to get to your wise mind *is* unblending! And you can use the following steps to help you further.

1. Assume that any painful or overwhelming thoughts and emotions are communications from parts (Fisher 2017). (Tip: Being aware of your triggers, discussed in chapter five, will help you be more prepared for parts activation in those situations.)

2. Rather than referring to parts' experiences as *yours* (as in, *I feel angry*), refer to these as belonging to the part (*There's a part of me that feels angry*). Notice what happens when you observe and nonjudgmentally describe *the parts'* experience—often people note a calmness, or sense of relief as the part feels validated.

3. See if you can create some space between yourself and the part so you still feel the parts' feelings, but less intensely, and you're able to feel yourself at the same time. A change in your body position (like a forward bend!), paced breathing, or looking at your hands to remind yourself of your current age can help. Continue to use parts language: *That part of me is feeling…* or *That part of me is thinking.*

4. From your wise mind, consider what the part needs: If this was your child, your friend, or your partner, what would you say or do for them? Depending on the age of the part, you might ask, *What do you need to help you feel less (angry, afraid, ashamed, etc.) right now?* If this is a child part, asking might not be appropriate—a five-year-old can't usually articulate what they need! So, ask yourself, *If this was a five-year-old child with me right now, feeling afraid, what would I do or say?* Then, go ahead and try it: for instance, imagine yourself having that conversation with your sixteen-year-old self or feel yourself hugging that five-year-old child. Don't just think the words or visualize the hug but try to really feel the emotion behind the words and feel the hug with your body, sending the message with your whole self. Then notice if the part responds. If you don't get a positive response, you can try again—maybe the part hears your words but doesn't *feel* them, or perhaps this part struggles to trust and it will take time to build a relationship with them. If the part is responsive, notice what it's like for you that the part feels soothed, reassured, calmer, or whatever their experience was.

Let's return to Marguerite for an example of unblending with a part.

Marguerite Unblending

Marguerite identified several parts in her system, including a nine-year-old submit part who would do whatever she could to please others. Marguerite recognized that this part (who she called "Nine") was trying to protect her—she had learned to submit to her brother and her parents in order to survive—but Nine's people-pleasing was now preventing Marguerite from finding healthy and fulfilling relationships. Nine didn't realize the trauma was over, they were now safe, and the behavior that once helped protect the system was now damaging.

Through practicing mindfulness, Marguerite became familiar with the triggers for Nine's people-pleasing behavior and she began recognizing when this part was becoming activated—her breathing became shallow; she felt sudden, intense shame; and her body language changed, almost as though she was trying to make herself smaller. Marguerite learned to validate Nine—telling her that her shame used to help keep her safe, but that the abuse wasn't her fault and she had nothing to feel ashamed about. Marguerite worked hard to show Nine that she cared about her; that Marguerite was no longer nine years old but an adult; that they were no longer living in the family home with her abusive family, so Nine no longer had to submit to others to keep them safe; and that, as the adult in the system, it was actually Wise Marguerite's job to keep them safe, not a nine-year-old child's! Marguerite still finds herself blended with Nine at times, but this happens less often, and she finds it easier to unblend, reassuring that young child that she's safe and taken care of.

Orienting Parts

I've mentioned that trauma parts often live in trauma time, and don't realize the trauma is over and they're safe now, because they don't *feel* safe (remember, when you've experienced ongoing trauma, your ANS has likely been trained to neurocept signals around you as dangerous when they're not). Orienting parts to time increases feelings of safety, security, and calm. For example, recall Cory with the twelve-year-old suicidal part: we had to remind that part, over and over again, that Cory was no longer twelve but thirty years old, he no longer lives at home with his parents, and he makes his own choices now. Here are some other strategies we used to orient that part to time:

- What's your address now? And where did you live when you were twelve years old?

- Who do you live with now? And who did you live with when you were twelve?

- Look at your hands—do they look like twelve-year-old hands? Or thirty-year-old hands?

- Notice how your body feels as you sit on the chair: can you feel the length of your body from the top of your head to the tips of your toes? Does this match with how tall you were, at the age of twelve?

- Does that twelve-year-old part know what year it is? What have you done in your life since you were twelve? (Gone to college? Worked in certain jobs? Moved? Gotten married? Adopted a pet? Had children?)

Think of ways to orient your parts—the trick is to find what works for you, and sometimes for each part. Make some notes here about things you do already that help orient your parts, and what you're willing to try:

_____

_____

_____

_____

_____

_____

One thing I find helpful in working with parts—my own and my clients—is to remember that we're trying to build healthy relationships with these parts of ourselves, and relationships take time and effort. That young part of you might not have gotten their needs met back then, but you can meet those needs now and, in this way, you're coming to terms with your trauma. Likewise, if your traumas occurred in adulthood, you can meet the needs *now* of your adult self that went through the trauma *then*.

Let's turn now to a DBT skill to help you come to terms with your trauma: acknowledging reality as it is.

Acknowledging Reality

In DBT, this skill is known as reality acceptance (Linehan 2014), but I've come to refer to it as *acknowledging reality* to help people understand that this isn't about liking or approving of something, or even being okay with it; we're simply acknowledging reality as it is. Let's start by looking at how this skill will be helpful, through an exercise.

Activity: Acknowledging Reality

Think of a difficult situation, either from your past or something that's ongoing in the present, that you're no longer fighting but have accepted or acknowledged. Here are some examples: going through a separation or divorce; not getting a job you really wanted; losing a friendship. Give that situation a title and write it here:

_____

Next, think about what it was like when that situation first happened (or, if it's an ongoing situation, when it first started); compare that to what it's like for you now that you've acknowledged that reality. How did acknowledging reality change your experience? Check the responses that resonate for you and add your own thoughts in the space provided.

- ☐ The situation has less power over you.

- ☐ You think about the situation less often.

- ☐ It's not as painful when you think about the situation now.

- ☐ You're more able to move on, or let go.

- ☐ You're more focused on the future.

- ☐ There's a sense of relief, peace, or calm regarding the situation.

- ☐ You feel like a weight has been lifted.

- ☐ You can focus more on what to do about the situation.

- ☐ _____

- ☐ _____

- ☐ _____

Hopefully, you can see how acknowledging reality will be helpful for you in the future based on this experience. It can take a lot of energy and hard work to acknowledge reality, especially when you have CPTSD, which inherently means there's a lot in your life to work on acknowledging in your recovery; recognizing how this will help can motivate you to practice, even when it seems difficult or even impossible. But you get to choose when you want to practice this skill, so if you're not feeling ready yet, there's lots of other work you can be doing in the meantime. If you do feel ready, keep reading.

Fighting Reality

The opposite of acknowledging reality is fighting reality (Linehan 2014). Human beings tend to judge, push away, or otherwise try to avoid things that cause us pain. Let's use Marguerite's trauma as an example of what fighting reality might look like:

- It shouldn't have happened; I shouldn't have been unsafe in my own home.

- It's not fair that my parents didn't protect me.

- I should have been able to stop the abuse.

- It's my fault.

While you might agree with some of Marguerite's statements ("Of course, it shouldn't have happened!"), this fighting reality thinking isn't helpful—it only increases suffering. Recall the skill of nonjudgmental stance from the last chapter, and how, when we judge, we inflame our emotions. The same happens when we're fighting reality.

Pain versus Suffering

In the context of this skill, we differentiate between pain, which consists of the inevitable, unavoidable emotions we all experience as human beings, and suffering, which involves the additional emotions we create when we refuse to acknowledge reality as it is. Think of Marguerite's situation: it makes sense that she'll feel anger, hurt, and sadness about the abuse she suffered—this is pain. But when we consider her fighting reality statements, you can probably see how this inflames her emotions and leads to suffering. For individuals with CPTSD, fighting reality is often associated with the symptom of negative self-view, which increases shame. For example, Marguerite's thought, *I should have been able to stop him*, will contribute to her suffering in the form of shame.

Like any DBT skill, acknowledging reality will not eliminate pain but it will reduce and gradually eliminate suffering, so that, over time, you'll only have the pain. When we can reduce or eliminate our suffering, there's more space for the pain, making it more bearable.

Steps to Acknowledging Reality

So, how do you get to the point of being able to acknowledge your reality? The first step is to consider what realities you need to work on accepting in your life. You might want to take some time right now to start a list of these, but be sure to write out the titles of the chapters rather than getting into details about each chapter (for example, Marguerite might note "abuse by my brother" as one experience she wants to accept). Once you're aware of what you want to work on, you can follow these steps to help you acknowledge the difficult situations in your life.

1. Choose one thing from your list to start with. It's a good idea to choose something less painful to begin; you can come back for the more painful situations when you're more comfortable with the skill. If you're struggling to decide where to start, or you don't feel ready to work on any of the situations on your list, think about other things you can practice with instead: being stuck in traffic, or the fact that it's raining on your day off. Then, make a commitment to yourself: as of right now, you're going to work on acknowledging this reality:

    _____

    _____

2. Notice when you're fighting that reality and make note of the fighting reality thoughts arising (*It shouldn't have happened, It's my fault, It's awful*):

    _____

    _____

3. Remind yourself of why you want to acknowledge this reality. (For example, *I know that acknowledging this reality will reduce my suffering, help me feel more at peace, and move on with my life.*) Then, ask yourself how you can talk back to that thought. Take a nonjudgmental perspective and change your fighting reality self-talk to acknowledging reality instead:

    _____

    _____

Then repeat steps two and three over and over again: Notice when you're fighting reality and turn your mind back to acknowledging reality as it is. I refer to this as the "internal argument," which is a normal part of the process of acknowledging reality—you'll waffle back and forth!

Because fighting reality can be very ingrained in your self-talk, you may want to write out some statements to read when you find yourself falling back into fighting reality; this will gradually help shift your thinking to acknowledging that this is your reality. Here are some statements Marguerite came up with to help her acknowledge the reality of her childhood:

- My brother abused me; I can't go back and change it, but it's in the past.

- The reality is I was just a kid—I had no ability to fight my brother off. I want to work on accepting this so I can live a healthier life.

- It wasn't my fault. My parents didn't protect me, but it's in the past and I'm safe now; I want to work on letting this go so I can move on with my life.

Now it's your turn: thinking of the situation you chose to work on first, write some statements that will help you stop fighting and instead acknowledge reality as it is:

- _____

  _____

- _____

  _____

- _____

  _____

Read these statements to yourself when the fighting reality thoughts arise, as well as regularly (every day, if possible!), to strengthen this new way of thinking.

Wrapping Up

In this chapter, you've had the opportunity to do some stage two work, begin to get to know and communicate with your parts, and learn some skills to help you work with them more effectively. I know this can be overwhelming—coming to terms with your trauma through parts work and skills like acknowledging reality typically takes a lot of energy. This is why the emphasis is on going slowly and taking a staged approach to treating CPTSD so you have a road map to recovery. Remember to go at your own pace and that trying to race to your destination will not necessarily get you there faster—or safely.

In the next chapter, we'll start looking at another typical challenge for individuals with CPTSD: relationships.

CHAPTER EIGHT

The Importance of Connections

You've been learning a lot about yourself and how the traumas you've experienced have contributed to the development of unhealthy patterns—such as in the way you think about yourself, or the behaviors you use to cope, and in your relationships (the focus of this chapter).

In chapter one, you learned that one of the symptoms of CPTSD is difficulties in relationships or feeling close to others. This often leads to avoidance of relationships or developing relationships with dynamics similar to those from past relationships—perhaps with abusive, controlling, or self-absorbed others. Hopefully, you're beginning to understand the many reasons for these difficulties: for instance, when you have a negative view of yourself, it's hard to believe others could care for you; when you don't feel safe with others, it's hard to let your guard down enough to form deep connections; or when the people closest to you have betrayed you, it's hard to trust this won't happen again in future.

In this chapter, we'll look at the importance of having connections with others and you'll have the opportunity to consider the relationships currently in your life, how healthy they are, and whether you need to increase connections with others. We'll also look at what it means to have healthy limits and I'll provide you with some tools to help you observe those limits, including skills for assertive communication and considerations for ending unhealthy relationships. These skills are not only often involved in stage three work but are also helpful in increasing safety and stability in stage one.

The Importance of Connections

Human beings are social creatures and are not meant to be alone. In fact, one study that looked at the consequences of loneliness and isolation found that a lack of social connection carried health risks similar to smoking fifteen cigarettes a day (Holt-Lunstad et al. 2015). In other words, this doesn't just affect our emotional health but our physical health.

With that said, I'd invite you to consider the following question from your wise mind: Do you think you have enough relationships in your life? Or is this something that's missing for you?

If you struggled to answer this question, here's an activity to help (based on Van Dijk 2022).

Activity: Assessing Your Connections

Write the names of the people to whom you feel closest. (It doesn't matter how often you see or talk to these people, just consider how close you feel to them.)

_____

_____

When you want to spend quality time with someone, who comes to mind? List everyone you can think of:

_____

_____

If you want to get out of the house and do something—catch a movie, go for coffee, take a walk—who can you call to keep you company?

_____

If you're feeling troubled, have a problem you're struggling with, or are in crisis, who are you comfortable talking to?

_____

Are there any groups you belong to through which you feel supported (like a support group or a spiritual or religious group)?

_____

Imagine yourself in crisis or struggling with intense emotions. If you have a go-to person (like a partner, parent, or best friend), imagine that person isn't available for some reason. Who could you turn to instead?

_____

Now imagine that person isn't available. Who else could you turn to?

_____

Take a moment to review your answers. Does anything stand out? Consider that question once more from your wise mind—do you think you have enough relationships in your life, or is this something that's missing? Write your thoughts here:

_____

_____

_____

_____

While everyone has different needs when it comes to connections with others, everyone does have these needs. As adult human beings, we can survive on our own, of course, but we thrive when we're part of a community.

Increasing Connections

You might not have found answering the previous question difficult, but doing something about it is often easier said than done. If you recognize you need more relationships, here are some ideas to consider.

Reconnecting

Consider people from your past with whom you could reconnect—people who are at least relatively emotionally healthy, that is! A friend from high school? An old neighbor? Even if you had a falling out with someone, it may be less complicated (and less scary) for you to attempt to restart that relationship. Write the names of people or any other thoughts you have here:

_____

_____

Strengthening Current Relationships

If reconnecting with others isn't an option, consider people currently in your life with whom you might work on forming a deeper connection: perhaps coworkers you've kept at arm's length or the person you keep seeing in your yoga class at whom you smile and say hello, but have never taken it further. Look around you to see who has the potential to become someone more meaningful in your life and consider what your first step might be (like striking up a conversation with the person in yoga or sitting with your coworker on break):

_____

_____

Creating New Connections

This tends to be the more difficult route as it typically involves putting yourself into new situations with the goal of meeting people who could become friends. Consider what new situations you might try: taking a pottery class, taking up a sport, or doing some volunteer work. Write any ideas that come to mind here:

_____

_____

Whatever activity you choose, the important thing is to make sure you look up—make eye contact with others. Smile. Do your best to be approachable and perhaps even push yourself to approach someone else and be friendly.

As you push yourself outside of your comfort zone, there are some things you'll need to keep in mind: some of your parts might not like this—for instance, it might not feel safe. You might find yourself in your yellow zone as your ANS detects signals of danger in environments that are unfamiliar and around people you don't know. Anxiety makes sense, so be sure to use the skills you've been learning to help with this. Our discussion in the next section regarding observing limits will also be helpful here.

Observing Limits

In DBT, *observing limits* (also referred to as *boundaries*) is the process of noticing whether someone's behavior is acceptable to you. Allowing someone to continue to behave toward you in ways you experience as unacceptable will usually result in feelings of resentment or burnout in the relationship. Here are some examples to get you thinking about your own limits:

- Matthew was out for dinner with his friend Liam. They were catching up and enjoying themselves when Liam made a disparaging comment about their waiter. Matthew was stunned but, not knowing how to respond, said nothing.

- Petra's sister Molly was unhappy in her relationship. Petra tried to be there to support Molly, but she refused to even try to make changes with her partner—she wouldn't talk to them about her unhappiness and she thought couples therapy was "a waste of time." Petra was sick of Molly just complaining all the time and not trying to change her situation and came to dread spending time with Molly, something she used to look forward to.

- Terrence loved his job working as a vet assistant, but he felt like his friend Maia took advantage of him by bringing her dogs for a "visit" on weekends so he could trim their nails. This felt like an intrusion on Terrence's time and he found himself growing resentful.

As you read these stories, do your own experiences come to mind? You might already be aware of some limits you struggle to observe (or perhaps you don't struggle at all, which is great!). Keep in mind that if you have CPTSD, it's not unusual to be unaware of your limits, to feel like you're not allowed to have wants or needs in relationships with others, or to struggle to communicate your limits to others. If this is a problem for you, consider times when you've found yourself judging someone's behavior or perhaps you've noticed feeling angry (or frustrated, irritated, resentful, and so on) in response to their behavior. Can you identify what the limit was that you weren't observing? Write your thoughts here:

_____

_____

_____

The first step in observing limits is becoming aware that something isn't okay for you; your emotions will often be a good indicator of this: notice resentment and other emotions on the anger spectrum (and yes, mindfulness will help with this!). Then, do your best not to judge and not assume the other person knows their behavior is problematic for you. Everyone has different limits, and these can also change depending on circumstances. You may not even be aware of a certain limit until you experience it being pushed, so how can you expect others to know what your limits are? What's important is that you learn to notice when it happens and then observe the limit by assertively communicating it to the other person. Let's return to our earlier examples to demonstrate.

- Matthew valued his friendship with Liam, but decided he didn't want to continue the friendship if Liam's behavior didn't change. He called Liam and told him how he felt and asked if Liam was willing to work on changing his behavior so they could remain friends.

- Petra told Molly she loved her and wanted to support her and shared how difficult it was to listen to her vent without trying to change her situation. She set a limit with Molly that, from now on when they were together, she could vent for five minutes before Petra would change the topic.

- Terrence decided to let Maia know that, to improve his self-care, he was going to start limiting the amount of work he did outside of his actual work hours. He was still willing to help her, but it would have to be on his schedule, not hers.

Once you've identified a limit you need to observe, the next step is communicating it to others. Easier said than done, I know, especially if you've learned it's not safe to express your needs and wants, that others' needs take priority over yours, or other similar things. This is where assertiveness comes in.

The Importance of Healthy Communication

Being unable to communicate effectively is one of the most common relationship problems. With a history of complex trauma, this may be related to parts becoming activated with intense emotions like anxiety (*What if they leave because I'm asking for too much?*) or shame (*I don't deserve to ask for this* or *I'm selfish*). It may be because you've never learned the skills to communicate assertively—perhaps because caregivers didn't have these skills themselves or because it was safer *not* to communicate physical and emotional needs. It could also be related to an inability to recognize that you have an unmet need, also not uncommon in CPTSD. Whatever the reason for difficulties in communication, the results are the same: your wants and needs remain unattended to, likely resulting in heightened emotions over time, increasing the likelihood of problematic behaviors—these might be avoidance behaviors such as substance use or self-harm, or they may be directed at the other person (like lashing out), which damage the relationship.

Rather than continue to fall into this pattern, however, you can choose to start working on healthy communication.

Assertiveness: What It Is and What Gets in the Way

Being *assertive* means clearly expressing yourself in a way that's respectful of yourself as well as others. Assertiveness involves caring about the other person and their needs, trying to see their perspective, and negotiating and compromising in an attempt to meet their needs as well as your own.

I mentioned earlier that people sometimes struggle with assertiveness because they don't feel deserving of having their needs met, or of saying no to the requests of others (individuals who experienced abuse or neglect in childhood have often been trained to believe their needs don't matter); negative self-perceptions (such as *I'm worthless*) may also contribute to this. But asserting yourself will gradually lead to feelings of self-respect and self-esteem—by *acting as though* you're deserving, you'll start to believe you *are* deserving. Being assertive will also improve your relationships, which will contribute to you feeling better about yourself.

How to Be Assertive

The first step in being assertive is deciding from your wise mind what your goals are. If you're not clear on what you'd like from the interaction, you'll struggle to communicate this to others. Let's look at Matthew as an example.

Matthew's Goal

Matthew realized that Liam's behavior at dinner went against his value of treating others respectfully, as he would want to be treated. His first thought was that he shouldn't be friends with Liam—he didn't want to associate with someone who would treat others that way. But as Matthew considered this, he was able to access his wise mind and realized his initial reaction was emotion-minded, coming from a younger part that had developed when he was being bullied in school. That part thought Liam was bad and wanted to cut him out of Matthew's life. From his wise self, however, Matthew acknowledged there were many qualities he liked about Liam—that's why they had been friends for such a long time. Matthew decided, instead of cutting Liam off (which was something he would have done in the past), he would tell him how he felt about his behavior and ask him to make a change.

The following are some DBT skills to help you be assertive (Linehan 2014). I'll outline the skills first, then we'll use Matthew as an example of how to put them into practice.

Describe the situation: Begin by describing the situation you want to discuss, sticking to the facts, and staying away from judgments and blaming. Think of this as telling the other person what the conversation is about.

Describe thoughts and emotions: Describe your thoughts and emotions about the situation (emotions are optional if it doesn't seem appropriate—for example, if the conversation is with your boss). Using "I" statements (for example, *I felt angry when you said that*) can be helpful and make it less likely that others will become defensive.

Clearly state what you want: Be specific about what you're asking for. This is where it's important to be certain of your goals so you can be clear about your request. Remember that others can't read your mind!

Reinforce: It's helpful if you can think of something the other person will get out of giving you what you're asking for. This is meant to motivate others to want to help as they see it's not all about you but that you're willing to give in order to get.

Let's look at how Matthew used these skills to have a conversation with Liam.

Describe the situation: When we were at dinner last weekend, you made a disrespectful comment about our waiter.

Describe thoughts and emotions: I found your comment offensive, and I felt angry.

Clearly state what you want: When we're together, I'd like you to be respectful of others and not to share your judgmental thoughts about them with me.

Reinforce: This will help me be more comfortable when we get together and will allow us to remain friends.

Now it's your turn. Think of a conversation you'd like (or need) to have with someone. This could be anything: asking your cell phone provider to change your plan, asking your best friend to change your weekend plans, or asking your partner to help you with an errand. In the space provided, write out your script. Tip: You can also use these skills to say no to a request someone is making of you. You might not need to include all the steps we've just looked at, but when saying no, it can be helpful to state your thoughts and emotions and to clearly state what you want—in this case, to say no.

Activity: Communicating Assertively

Describe the situation: _____

_____

Describe thoughts and emotions: _____

_____

Clearly state what you want: _____

_____

Reinforce: _____

_____

I'd strongly recommend you rehearse your script once you've written it; of course, you can't script an entire conversation with someone as you can't be certain of their responses but rehearsing how you'd like to start the conversation will build your confidence in these new skills. If it feels too hard to have the conversation right now, you might read the script to start (especially if it's a conversation with someone you're close to, who knows about your CPTSD and the work you're doing). Over time, as you continue to practice, your confidence will grow, and being assertive—like any skill—will start to come more naturally to you.

Additional Skills for Assertiveness

These additional skills for assertiveness will help you get your needs met and make it more likely that you'll maintain relationships and feel good about yourself after you've been assertive (Linehan 2014).

Mindfulness

I often hear people refer to themselves as "conflict avoidant," they avoid having difficult conversations with people in their life, often out of fear of losing the person or damaging the relationship. I remind my clients that, right now, *it's a conversation, not a conflict*. The "conflict" is the imaginary scenario you've created in your mind—it's not reality; remembering this will help reduce your anxiety.

Being mindful in interactions is also typically experienced as validating for others, as it communicates that you're paying attention and are interested in them and the conversation. Eliminate distractions: put down your phone, turn off the TV, and give the person your full attention. As best as you can, focus on what they're saying (rather than, for instance, what your response will be), ask questions, and be interested in their answers. While you might find this difficult for a variety of reasons (like, connecting with others is scary!), it typically goes a long way in improving relationships—and remember how important it is to have connections with others.

Validating Others

In chapter six, you learned the skill of self-validation and I've mentioned the importance of validating your parts as well. See if you can bring to mind a time when someone validated you: can you recall how it felt? Usually, it's soothing or calming to be understood and accepted; it brings down the intensity of emotions. It can also help increase our sense of connection with the person we're validating. This is how validation helps in our relationships with others (and keep in mind that validating others doesn't necessarily mean that you agree with or like what you're validating!).

Be Genuine and Use Humor

Being assertive doesn't necessarily mean you have to be all serious. If it's appropriate, lightening the mood of an important or difficult conversation by using humor, smiling, and laughing can help reduce tension, improving the likelihood of a positive outcome.

And if you haven't yet noticed, all the skills we've discussed so far in this chapter can also improve relationships within your self-system, so you can be thinking not just about using these skills with the people around you but with your parts!

What to Do About Unhealthy Relationships

People with CPTSD commonly find themselves in unhealthy relationships—perhaps with those who are abusive or neglectful or maybe just with others who are emotionally unhealthy and with whom they've developed unhealthy patterns (such as having an imbalanced relationship where one person enables the other's self-destructive behaviors). Part of the problem if you have a history of trauma—especially if this involved childhood trauma—is that you likely didn't have many examples of healthy relationships and you didn't learn to detect the red flags others might see when they haven't grown up with abuse.

Before we look at how to end unhealthy relationships, let's look at some of the things that might indicate a relationship is actually unhealthy.

Red Flags

While I can't provide an exhaustive list of the things to be on the lookout for in your friendships or romantic relationships, here are some things you can consider:

- **Physical abuse:** If someone is physically aggressive toward you—hitting, kicking, pushing, or any other kind of physical contact; or threatening to do any of these things—this is a physically abusive situation. It's not safe.

- **Sexual abuse:** No one has the right to physically force you, or emotionally coerce you, to have any kind of sexual contact with them. This is abuse.

- **Emotional abuse** is any act that detracts from your sense of identity, dignity, and self-worth. Examples include verbal abuse: name-calling, threatening, or yelling; attempts to control, isolate, or monitor a person's behavior; or humiliating or shaming a person. Feeling afraid of someone or walking on eggshells are indicators that you may be in an abusive relationship.

- **Dishonesty:** If you discover someone hasn't been honest with you (without good reason), red flag. What's "a good reason" though? I teach my clients that sometimes it makes sense to choose to lie from our wise mind. If you're on a first date with someone and they ask why it's been so long since you've been in a relationship, you might not feel comfortable sharing that your last partner was abusive, so it makes sense to tell them you've been prioritizing your career. Or at a job interview, you're not sure if it's safe to share that you have CPTSD and this has prevented you from working for the last couple of years—I'd suggest it's okay to say you're between jobs trying to figure out what you want to do. If you find out the person you've just started dating lied to you about being with their ex because they thought you might get angry—that's not a good reason to lie. Red flag.

- **Substance use:** If someone is misusing drugs or alcohol, this is a red flag as it puts you in danger of many of the other red flags, including abuse and emotional disconnection. Someone misusing substances is not living a healthy lifestyle. Reconsider your involvement.

These red flags are good cause to consider ending a relationship, which we'll look at shortly. But there may also be times when these red flags aren't present and the relationship is problematic in other ways: perhaps you feel unsatisfied and you're beginning to realize your needs aren't being met, you feel stuck in the relationship out of a sense of obligation or misplaced loyalty, or maybe you have very few relationships so you don't want to lose this one. If a relationship is important to you and it isn't abusive or somehow destructive, ending it should be a last resort: when you've used all of your skills, and nothing is changing. Let's explore important aspects of ending a relationship.

Make a Wise Choice

Don't let your parts make the choice for you—remember to assume that any intense emotion is a communication from a part, and if you make the decision while you're blended, you're likely to regret that emotion-minded decision later. You might choose to go to your meeting place where you can have a discussion with your parts about this decision and all parts can weigh in, but the decision should come from your wise self. Completing a cost-benefit analysis from chapter four can also be helpful here.

Safety First!

Remember that everyone has the right to be physically and emotionally safe and respected, so if you're in a relationship (romantic, friendship, family, or otherwise) in which you're being abused in any way, you have the right—and even owe it to yourself!—to leave. If you're not sure how to do this or if you need extra support around relationships generally, ask someone you trust for help or call your local crisis line or shelter.

Wrapping Up

Relationships can be difficult enough to navigate when you don't have a history of trauma—add CPTSD (often involving relational trauma) into the mix and it makes sense you'll struggle in this area.

In this chapter, you've hopefully started to learn more about why you have the struggles you do in relationships, set some goals for yourself regarding the connections (or lack of) in your life, and learn some skills that will help you work toward your relationship goals. Remember, it makes sense that parts may be triggered when thinking about relationships and how to be more skillful in them, so continue to work with those aspects of yourself; also remember that many of the skills we've discussed in this chapter can actually be used with your parts to enhance communication and cooperation.

In the next chapter, we'll discuss the importance of actively working to increase positive experiences and pleasurable emotions in your life.

CHAPTER NINE

How to Increase the Pleasure in Your Life

So far in this workbook, we've looked at different ways of understanding your difficult experiences—such as dissociation, target behaviors, and problems in relationships—and skills to help you manage the emotional pain related to CPTSD. In this chapter, we're going to switch gears and focus not on ways of reducing the pain but on building more positive experiences in your life to increase pleasurable emotions.

Focusing on the positive and increasing pleasure in your life might sound great, but once you start working on it, you might find you struggle with this (or parts of you do!), especially if you're in stage one of your trauma treatment journey. That may sound strange, but when you've experienced prolonged periods of not being safe, times of calm, peace, and contentment can feel uncomfortable or even frightening. You've become accustomed to living in the yellow and red zones, or your parts get used to constantly being on guard in order to keep you safe. So, if you notice you struggle with this chapter, rest assured, this isn't uncommon. And as I've said so many times already, take all the time you need and be patient with yourself as you do this work. If you've done trauma resolution work, the skills we'll be looking at here will help with your stage three (integration) work; otherwise, these can also be helpful in stage one.

To ease you in, let's start with a skill you've already learned and are hopefully practicing: mindfulness.

Be Mindful of the Positives

It can be easy to overlook pleasurable feelings that arise, such as calm, peace, or contentment, since they're not as intense as the pain you may be used to experiencing or if they're fleeting moments of pleasure. When life is chaotic and busy, or when you're experiencing intense emotions regularly, it can be hard to even notice the roses, never mind remember to stop and smell them! Think about moments in your life that might give you some kind of little pleasure if you could only see it: your dog greeting you at the door with excitement and unconditional love, looking out your window at the snow quietly falling, the sun shining, or hugging someone you care about.

Practicing mindfulness will help you notice the pleasure in your life, even when it's there for just a short time, or when the emotion isn't an intense one like happiness or joy. Slowing yourself down and noticing these moments will not only help you increase the pleasure you experience in life but will also lead to an increased sense of well-being.

Activities to Increase Pleasurable Emotions

First, let's clarify what I mean by *pleasure*. If you haven't experienced emotions like happiness or joy very often in your life, or if it's been a long time since you've felt these emotions, it might be unrealistic to expect to experience these emotions in the short term. To help you think more broadly, consider the following list of pleasurable emotions.

Calm	Peaceful	Soothed	Content
Satisfied	Relaxed	Gratified	Comfortable
Restful	Proud	Enjoyment	Amused
Safe	Appreciative	Interest	Curious

If there are other words that describe pleasure for you, write them in the blanks:

_____   _____   _____

_____   _____   _____

It can also be helpful to know that you might experience a pleasurable emotion combined with an uncomfortable (or even distressing) emotion, such as feeling anxious while you're enjoying yourself, or feeling dread about the happiness you're experiencing (that idea of foreboding joy we discussed in chapter five). This often makes perfect sense in the context of CPTSD: for example, it might not have been safe to express any emotion with an abusive caregiver, or perhaps a negative self-view causes you to question if you're deserving of feeling pleasure. Whatever the cause of your difficulty with the pleasurable emotion, mindfulness will help you come back to the present moment and allow yourself to be with the pleasurable emotion with your full attention, and with acceptance. As you continue to practice this, over time, you should notice that your discomfort with experiencing pleasure decreases.

To help you be mindful of those pleasurable emotions, however, you first have to find ways of generating them! Following is a list of activities that change our body chemistry to help us feel some kind of pleasure. Since everyone's experience of these activities will be different, I'd invite you to try each of these to find which ones work best for you.

Be in nature. Just twenty minutes of being in nature can significantly reduce stress. A study by Beil and Hanes (2013) compared one group of people sitting in a city park with no trees to a second group who sat in the woods; they found that the group exposed to nature reported significantly less stress and an eightfold decrease in a biological marker of stress known as salivary alpha-amylase.

Activate your vagus nerve. As you learned in chapter three, activating the vagus nerve helps to bring you into the green zone, where you'll be more able to connect with others, mindfully engage in the present moment, and get to a calmer state. Remember that the vagus nerve is connected to our vocal cords, so humming, chanting a mantra, gargling, laughing, or singing can also help generate pleasurable emotions.

Singing with others has the additional benefit of generating oxytocin—also known as the "love hormone"—because it helps us feel more connected to others. Oxytocin also helps calm the amygdala, the part of the brain that's primarily involved in the processing of emotions and memories associated with fear, and temporarily prevents the release of stress hormones.

Touch (hugging, holding hands with others, even petting your dog, cat, or guinea pig) also releases oxytocin and reduces stress and feelings of loneliness. And laughing with others also has added benefits in reducing stress and increasing pleasure, so here's a reminder of the importance of connecting with others!

Listen to music. Research has found that another chemical called dopamine—known as the "feel-good neurotransmitter"—is released in the brain when we listen to music we enjoy, so put on your favorite tunes. And singing along will further enhance your enjoyment as you stimulate your vagus nerve!

These are activities that change your body chemistry in some way to help you experience pleasurable emotions, but these are just a starting point. Let's look at what other activities you can do to increase pleasure in your life.

Activity: Experimenting with Pleasurable Activities

Many people with CPTSD didn't have the opportunity as children to explore different activities to learn what they like and dislike. Or, if your CPTSD is related to adult trauma, you might feel like you've lost yourself and no longer have a sense of what brings you enjoyment. Either way, I think of this as an experiment you have to do now: to figure out what will bring you pleasure.

Start by listing any (healthy) activities you've done in the past that generated some kind of pleasurable emotions. Remember, we might not be talking "enjoyment" or "fun" but perhaps calm, content, relaxed, at peace, curious, and so on:

_____

_____

_____

_____

If you're having difficulties, I'd invite you to return to the list of activities from chapter four to help you brainstorm about what might be pleasurable for you. As you read through the list, put a check beside any activities you'd be willing to try and think about how you might modify these activities to suit you better.

If you're still struggling to think of activities to try, consider anything that's ever appealed to you; keep in mind that you're just brainstorming right now, so the sky's the limit! For example, maybe you saw a show about scuba diving and that caught your interest—write it down. Or perhaps you have a friend who plays a sport that sounds fun—add it to the list. Ask family and friends for suggestions or Google "fun things to do" or "enjoyable activities" and get some ideas to add to your list.

Add anything else you can think of:

_____

_____

_____

_____

_____

Once you've got your list, choose an activity to start with. You might find that some things on your list aren't realistic in the short term—maybe scuba diving is too expensive for you right now. While starting a new hobby can be enjoyable, planning for it can also give you pleasure, so consider how you might be able to work toward doing an activity that seems out of reach in the short term. For example, start reading about scuba diving and marine life; find a local dive shop where you can talk to people about the sport; or work on improving your swimming at the local pool. Saving up for an activity can also give you a sense of satisfaction, and if you have someone you can share your adventure with, talking about the activity and making plans together also generates pleasure. Make some notes here about which activity you'd like to try first (or work toward), and what you'll do:

_____

_____

_____

_____

_____

_____

The next step is to get started and be mindful of the pleasure you'll hopefully notice arising. We're not quite done with options for generating pleasurable emotions, though.

Living by Your Values

A *value* is a core, fundamental belief or principle that helps us decide what's important and drives our attitudes and behaviors. Living life according to your values can help reduce painful emotions such as guilt and shame and will often result in some kind of pleasure as well, allowing you to live life more freely, increase self-confidence, and provide a sense of satisfaction, peace, contentment, or potentially even happiness and joy at times. This can be difficult, however, when you've experienced developmental trauma and you've been so busy focusing on survival that you weren't able to develop a sense of who you are and what's important to you. Or, if you've developed CPTSD as an adult, this can cause you to lose sight of these things. Either way, doing some work to identify your values will help you in the ways I've already described, as well as by aiding you in accessing your wise mind.

Here are some examples of values; circle the ones you identify with and add any others that are important to you.

Authenticity	Achievement	Adventure	Autonomy
Balance	Compassion	Community	Creativity
Determination	Faith	Growth	Honesty
Humor	Justice	Kindness	Leadership
Loyalty	Peace	Respect	Responsibility
Spirituality	Stability	Trustworthiness	Wisdom

_____   _____   _____

_____   _____   _____

Of the values you've identified as important, put a check beside the ones you believe you're currently living your life according to and put an X beside those areas that need attention. Keep these in mind for when we look at setting goals, shortly.

Experiencing and expressing gratitude might also be a value for you; this is one that comes with additional benefits.

Expressing Gratitude

Expressing gratitude—being thankful for someone or something—can also lead to, and enhance our capacity for, pleasurable emotions. While the idea of developing a gratitude practice has become a bit of a pop-culture cliché, it does have merit! Research has shown that gratitude contributes to our emotional health, increasing well-being, resilience, compassion, and satisfaction in life; strengthens relationships; and reduces stress and depression (Emmons and McCullough 2003; Sheldon and Lyubomirsky 2007).

There's also evidence that gratitude can have positive effects on physical health, including contributing to the prevention of cardiovascular disease through changes in inflammation and functions of the ANS and other systems in the body (Wang et al. 2023) and improving sleep quality (Wood et al. 2009). These benefits for our physical health, of course, will contribute to improved mental and emotional health, so this becomes a lovely, healthy cycle!

Gratitude often arises spontaneously, but as you can see, there are many reasons to make it an intentional practice as well as to strengthen the brain's neural circuits for this emotion—in other words, the more we practice it consciously, the more we'll spontaneously be able to experience it. So, how do you practice gratitude? The key is in noticing it (yep, mindfulness once again), and then finding ways to express it. Here are some ideas:

Keep a gratitude journal. Every day, write three things you're grateful for. This could be the fact that you have a roof over your head, that it didn't rain on your walk to work, or that you made it out of the abusive situation you were living in.

Create a gratitude jar. A different spin on the gratitude journal, you can create a gratitude jar (or box) where each day you write down one thing on a piece of paper and put it into the jar; periodically, you can revisit your jar to "count your blessings" and remind yourself of the things in life for which you're grateful.

Write a letter of gratitude. Write a letter to someone (you don't necessarily have to send it!) expressing your gratitude to them for something they've done, or for the effect they've had on your life. This could be someone from your present or your past (it might even be someone who's no longer alive). It might be a friend or family member, a current or ex-partner, therapist, mentor, teacher, coworker, or your pet. It could be someone you've never met, but who had a profound impact on your life in some way. Again, it doesn't matter if you send the letter—what matters is that you express your gratitude.

Be mindful when someone is thanking you, giving you a compliment, or saying something else that makes you feel good. Notice if this is difficult for you (this may be a part); if so, do your best to just notice the emotions arising and validate the part of yourself that's struggling to accept what's being offered. If this isn't difficult for you (yay!), be mindful of this experience.

Keep a gratitude photo journal. Every day, take a photograph of something for which you're grateful. You might choose to post it to social media to share your gratitude with others—or you might not! What's important is that you're making note of your feelings of gratitude in an intentional way. It's also helpful that you can go back and review those photos—this can become part of your enjoyable activities practice as well!

I've given you lots of options here for generating pleasurable emotions, but if you're still struggling to think of activities that might give you some kind of pleasure, the next section on goal-setting might also help.

Setting Goals

As with pleasurable activities, people with CPTSD can struggle with goal-setting for a number of reasons: perhaps you were too busy trying to survive the present to think about the future, or it wasn't safe to hope that you might even *have* a future. If you're in stage one of trauma treatment, you might need to look at setting goals to help increase your stability. Or, if you've already done trauma resolution work and you've moved into stage three (integration), this section will help you consider what you'd like life after trauma to look like.

Having goals not only gives us a direction in life but we also usually experience a sense of pride in ourselves when we reach a goal; having goals gives us something to look forward to, even if we don't achieve all of them. Not having goals—a sense of who you'd like to be, where you'd like to be, what you'd like to be doing, and so on—can leave you feeling unmoored and without direction. Not having something you're working toward can lead to a lack of fulfillment and feeling stuck. So, what are your goals? Don't worry if you're not sure; in the next activity, you'll have the opportunity to consider this.

Activity: Considering Your Goals

Consider where you'd like to see yourself in the next six months, one year, five years. What would you like for yourself? To be able to manage emotions more effectively? Do stage two therapy to help you resolve your traumas? Live your life according to your values? Go back to school to work toward a fulfilling career? Take better care of your physical health? Eliminate certain unhealthy relationships from your life? Remembering the sky is the limit, write down any goals that come to mind:

_____

_____

_____

_____

_____

_____

If you're stuck, ask yourself the question, *What would I do if I had six months to live?* If that was the case, what would you want to change in your life? This can help put things into perspective!

Once you've come up with some goals, choose one you'd like to start with—it might be hard to choose just one, but working on more than one goal at a time can be overwhelming, so I wouldn't advise it. Remember, you can come back to work on the others later. It can also help to choose a less complex goal to start. When you've decided on one goal, break it down into smaller steps. For example, if my goal is to have healthier relationships, I might break it down into these steps:

1.   Assess the relationships in my life currently: Are they balanced? Am I getting my wants met? Am I happy with the quality of them?

2.   Make a list of the relationships I want to change; choose one relationship to start.

3.   Ask myself: Is this an abusive relationship that I need to end or is it a relationship that's important to me? Do I want to improve it?

4.   If I want to keep the relationship, the next step is to ask myself: what needs to change for it to become healthier?

5.   Then I ask myself: what's one thing I can do in the short term to start changing the relationship? (for example, have a conversation with the person about what needs to change)

6.   I then figure out what skills I need to use and make plans to implement that first step.

In this example, you see how I've taken a long-term goal and broken it down into smaller steps that I can work toward in the short term. Now see if you can do the same for the goal you've chosen to start with. Remember that if you're struggling, you can ask someone you trust for help.

Wrapping Up

In this chapter, we looked at some ways to generate pleasurable emotions by creating more opportunities for positive events—changing the body's chemistry, experimenting with activities that might be pleasurable, examining values, practicing gratitude, and setting goals. Remember that managing the pain related to your CPTSD isn't enough—you also have to build a life worth living for yourself, and part of this is finding ways to experience pleasure.

In the next chapter, we'll revisit the idea of stage two work to help you decide if you want to engage in trauma resolution therapy by looking at some of the treatments currently being used to treat PTSD and, by extension, CPTSD so you'll be more prepared to make decisions around this.

CHAPTER TEN

Next Steps

My goal in this book has been to help you learn ways of managing your CPTSD through understanding your symptoms and using skills. In this final chapter, we'll look at what your next steps might be on your journey to recovery, including reevaluating where you are now and looking at some of the reasons you might want to move into stage two treatment. We'll also look at some considerations for working with a therapist and I'll provide some information about several of the commonly used treatments for PTSD, and by extension, CPTSD.

Considerations for Stage Two Treatment

While a unifying theme of trauma-focused therapies is revisiting the trauma, this doesn't necessarily mean reexperiencing it, but it will involve getting in touch with trauma-related emotions, thoughts, and beliefs that you have developed about yourself and the world as a result of the trauma. Trauma resolution means being able to integrate the traumatic experiences into your life story, understanding that this is an event that happened to you and that it happened in the past. It means allowing yourself to grieve for what you've lost and learning to build a life worth living despite the traumas. Let's review some other benefits of doing this work.

Reducing Anxiety and Avoidance

You've learned previously that anxiety and avoidance are symptoms of CPTSD. This saps your energy and reduces the size of your world as you avoid people, places, and things that remind you of the traumas in your attempts to keep yourself safe. Engaging in stage two work can help you confront the trauma memories and overcome your fears, allowing you to build a life worth living that includes healthy coping skills and increased self-esteem and self-confidence.

Challenging Negative Beliefs

Having negative beliefs about yourself (like *I'm bad*) is another common symptom of CPTSD; beliefs such as these will typically increase painful emotions such as shame and anger toward yourself. Trauma resolution will help you change these beliefs and develop more balanced thinking (such as *I was a child, it wasn't my fault*), thereby reducing those painful emotions.

Trauma also results in negative beliefs about others and the world quite often, especially when the trauma has been relational in nature, as is so often the case with CPTSD. These negative beliefs naturally result in an inability to feel safe and make it difficult to trust others. Through trauma resolution work, someone who developed the belief *It's not safe to trust* gradually shifts this belief to something more balanced, such as, *I can learn to trust others and keep myself safe*. Shifts in perspectives such as these will go a long way in helping you to expand your world, connect with others, and move forward from the traumatic events.

The Experience of Validation

People who have experienced trauma have often tried to tell others about their experiences and have been met with denial, blame, minimization, or other invalidating responses, which adds additional layers to the trauma they've already experienced. Therapy can provide a safe and accepting environment to facilitate healing and growth. In addition, because CPTSD is so often the result of trauma that is relational in nature, the therapeutic relationship provides an opportunity for you to heal in the context of a healthy relationship, which is often very helpful for people in their recovery from this kind of trauma.

Let's help you assess your readiness for stage two work before we move into what you'll need to know about choosing a therapist.

What Stage Are You Ready for Now?

Recovering from trauma is a journey that you must take at your own pace. This next activity isn't about comparing yourself now to where you were when you began reading this workbook but it can be helpful to look at your roadmap periodically to ensure you're going where you want to go. So, take some time to go through the following questions to reassess what stage you're in and help you set goals for where you'd like to go next.

Stage One: Safety and Stabilization

1. Have you been using skills to reduce or eliminate destabilizing behaviors, such as self-harming, suicidal behaviors, substance use, disordered eating, or other self-destructive behaviors? Make some notes about how you're doing with not acting on urges, what skills have been helpful, what skills you need to work on using more, and so on:

   _____

   _____

2. Consider how you're doing with using skills to manage emotions: do you often feel out of control with emotions? For example, lashing out at others or having panic attacks or high anxiety. Make some notes here about how you're doing with using skills to help with this, what skills have been helpful, which ones you need to work on using more, and so on:

   _____

   _____

3. If you dissociate, how do you feel you're doing using skills to help reduce this tendency? Make some notes about which skills have been helpful, which ones you need to work on using more, and so on:

   _____

   _____

4. How have you been working toward increasing external stability in your life? For example, changes in housing or finances; eliminating relationships with others who are abusive; or reducing your exposure to environments in which you experience bullying, discrimination, or harassment. Make some notes here about what you still need to work on changing to increase your stability:

   _____

   _____

5. How have you been doing with meeting your basic health needs—for example, sleeping too much or too little, eating too much or too little, or using drugs or alcohol in unhealthy

ways? Make some notes here about what progress you've made, and what you still need to work on:

_____

_____

Review your answers and consider whether you think you need to continue to work on increasing your stability before you're ready to move to stage two. One of the modifications that must usually be made to treatments for PTSD when working with individuals with CPTSD is incorporating a longer stabilization stage of treatment, so please don't worry if you're not there yet! Moving into stage two before you're ready can undo the work you've been doing. Keep working on the skills you've been learning and be patient with yourself. If you find that dissociation is holding you back, or if you continue to have suicidal or self-harming thoughts and urges, consider connecting with a therapist.

If you're thinking you might be ready for stage two, move on to the next set of questions to determine if this would be helpful.

Stage Two: Trauma Resolution

1. When you think of the trauma you experienced, does it feel like it's still happening on some level in the present (even if you know logically it's not)?

    _____

2. Do you find yourself struggling in relationships with others? For example, avoiding relationships, often putting others' needs before your own, taking responsibility for others' emotions, or worrying that people will leave you?

    _____

3. When you think of the trauma, is there a sense of denial of the event, or imagining that it happened to someone else?

    _____

4. When you think of the trauma, do you find yourself thinking it's your fault, or believing it means something negative about you as a person?

    _____

If you answered no to these questions, you may be well on your way to recovery without engaging in stage two work, so feel free to move on to the questions about stage three or you can consider the questions in the next section. Remember that you now have skills and strategies to help you in stage three (including parts work, reality acceptance, and increasing pleasurable emotions and connections with others).

If you answered yes to any of these questions, you would likely benefit from stage two work. Keep in mind, however, that processing trauma is typically difficult work involving intense emotions as memories are processed. Therefore, ask yourself the following questions to help determine if you're ready for stage two:

1. What kind of support will you need from others? (For instance, help with childcare or other responsibilities? Additional emotional support?)

   _____

   _____

2. Who do you have in your life who will support you while you're doing this work?

   _____

   _____

3. Are you in good physical health? (For example, if you're currently undergoing medical testing for unexplained symptoms, this can be destabilizing.)

   _____

   _____

4. Do you currently have the time to commit to doing this work? (This will vary depending on what type of therapy you'll be doing, and the homework required.)

   _____

   _____

5. Do you currently have the financial means to commit to the full course of therapy?

   _____

   _____

If you've decided to move into stage two and you think you're ready for it based on your answers to these questions, be sure to continue using the skills you've learned, to maintain or even increase your stability for the work to come. If you're moving to stage two, you can skip the following section and look at considerations for trauma resolution.

Stage Three: Integration

The following questions will give you a better sense of what you still need to focus on in stage three. If you know you're not yet ready for this stage, I'd suggest you skip this part to avoid becoming overwhelmed thinking about the work to come later; remember, these issues may naturally be resolved through the work you do in trauma resolution.

1. Who are you now that the trauma is no longer holding you back? What do you want in your life to make it more worth living?

    _____

    _____

2. What are your values and beliefs? What's important to you in life?

    _____

    _____

3. What are your goals for the future?

    _____

    _____

4. What gives you a sense of fulfillment in life?

    _____

    _____

5. Are you happy with your current relationships? Do you have enough people in your life, and are these relationships healthy and satisfying?

_____

_____

6. Are there relationships you need to look at ending? If so, do you have the skills to end them?

_____

_____

Hopefully, you now have a clearer picture of what work you have left to do in stage three. Many of the skills in this workbook will help you work on these goals, but if you find yourself stuck, consider connecting with a therapist.

In this final section, we'll look at some things to consider if you're planning on moving into stage two. If you're not ready for this yet, I'd suggest you put the book aside for the time being and continue to work on stage one work.

Considerations for Trauma Resolution

Many mental health clinicians are trained in the treatment of PTSD, but CPTSD is typically much more complex, involving well-constructed defense mechanisms to protect individuals from further pain. Therefore, it's usually a good idea to look for a therapist who has experience with CPTSD.

Processing Trauma from Safety

Throughout this book, we've talked about the importance of developing safety and stability in your life as necessary preparation for trauma resolution. One reason for this is you must be able to maintain awareness of the present moment and understand you're safe in the here and now (in other words, your wise self is in charge and you're able to get to your green zone) for your entire internal system to understand that the trauma is truly over (Fisher 2017). Hopefully, you've been doing the work in this book that will increase internal stability (such as managing emotions; working on self-harming, suicidal, and other target behaviors; and developing cooperation between parts) as well as external stability (such as eliminating unsafe or abusive relationships and observing your limits with others). But you must also feel *safe enough* in a therapeutic relationship to do this type of work.

Generally, the quality of the relationship between therapist and client has a moderate influence on how well the therapy works (Meichenbaum 2017). In other words, if you have a good relationship with your therapist, in which you feel accepted and understood and you believe you can trust your therapist, you'll be more likely to benefit from therapy. Since CPTSD often involves relational trauma, it makes sense that trusting others may be one of the first challenges you face when starting therapy. Working with a therapist who's validating and calm (and therefore able to help you coregulate) will gradually allow you to build a sense of trust and will help you learn to feel safer. If you belong to the BIPOC and/or LGBTQ+ community, this means finding a therapist who's knowledgeable about the effects of oppression, discrimination, racism, and intergenerational trauma, and how these experiences contribute to trauma.

While you may not feel safe and able to trust your therapist right away (this might make perfect sense given your trauma, as your parts work to protect you), it's important you feel comfortable enough to work on developing a relationship with them. If your wise self doesn't feel understood, accepted, or believed by your therapist, find someone new to work with.

Of course, if you're already working with a mental health professional, they may be able to refer you to a specialist; if you're a veteran, depending on where you live, there may be organizations that offer therapy and resources for PTSD.

Trauma Processing Therapies

Given that CPTSD is a newly defined condition, research is limited but ongoing to determine which therapeutic approaches will be most effective in treating it; however, I'm certain the answer to this question will be *it depends*! Everyone is different, with diverse types of traumatic experiences, so it makes sense that different treatment modalities (and lengths of treatment) will be required, depending on individual circumstances and preferences. Until more research emerges, therapists are usually adapting evidence-based PTSD treatments for CPTSD combined with an extended stabilization phase to improve your ability to manage emotions, help you more accurately evaluate your thoughts, and increase your capacity for self-compassion.

The other piece that may contribute to your choice of therapist is if you prefer a specific treatment. In the next section, I'll describe some of the therapies commonly used to treat CPTSD, but please keep in mind that not all treatments will be appropriate for all individuals. When you start working with an effective trauma therapist, they'll work with you to decide which treatments will be most likely to benefit you.

Eye Movement Desensitization and Reprocessing (EMDR) Therapy

EMDR therapy was developed by psychologist Francine Shapiro in 1987 to help people heal from trauma and other distressing life experiences. The story goes that, as she was walking in the park one day, thinking of a distressing memory of her own, Shapiro realized that as her eyes shifted back and forth, the painful emotions associated with the memory decreased. She theorized the eye movements had a desensitizing effect, and in a trial using horizontal eye movements with individuals with PTSD, Shapiro found significant reductions in distress and increased ratings of confidence in a positive belief associated with the trauma. Thus, EMDR therapy was born!

It's widely accepted that memories of traumatic events are not encoded in our brains the same as nontraumatic memories. You'll often hear traumatic memories referred to as being *unprocessed*, *frozen*, or *undigested*, meaning they're unable to link up to other more adaptive information stored in the brain. EMDR therapy is based on the idea that our brain naturally moves toward health and healing: just as our body instinctively knows how to heal itself when we get a paper cut, our brain also has an *adaptive information processing* (AIP) system that helps us move toward psychological healing. And just as physical healing can be complicated at times—such as when the paper cut gets infected—and we have to help our body heal by using an antibiotic ointment, our brain sometimes needs a little help too. Occasionally, something so extraordinary happens that our system can't process it, leading to a trauma response. EMDR therapy is the antibiotic ointment that helps our brain do what it needs to heal: through use of dual attention stimulus (DAS), such as eye movements or tapping (for instance, on your shoulders or knees), traumatic material is linked to adaptive information, which reduces and gradually eliminates the effects of the trauma.

EMDR therapy is a very structured therapy and requires very specific training; be sure that the EMDR therapist you choose has a minimum of basic training with an organization accredited by the EMDR International Association (EMDRIA).

Prolonged Exposure (PE) Therapy

PE is a treatment for PTSD that, as the name suggests, involves confronting the source of your fear to reduce anxiety around it. Psychologists Edna Foa and Michael Kozak are the creators of this well-established, evidence-based treatment for PTSD. In 1986, they presented the theoretical framework behind PE, Emotion Processing Theory, which posits that memories store our emotional responses to the world. When we experience a traumatic event, new connections are created in our minds, causing an anxiety response to previously neutral events, objects, people, or memories (triggers). According to this theory, PTSD symptoms are exaggerated fear responses to a traumatic memory; avoidance of all the reminders of the traumatic event reinforces these symptoms and prevents us from having the opportunity to process the memory or learn that the triggers are not actually threatening.

PE helps change our response to these anxiety-provoking triggers in a safe and controlled manner through two methods: first, through imaginal exposure, where you revisit the trauma by recounting and imagining it; and second, through in vivo exposure, where you face the triggers that remind you of the trauma. The goal of PE is *habituation*: when you jump into a cold lake, it feels freezing at first, but after a few minutes, your body and brain habituate and it doesn't feel as cold anymore. In the same way, gradually exposing yourself to anxiety-provoking triggers long enough allows your system to learn there's nothing dangerous or threatening, and the anxiety isn't warranted.

Cognitive Processing Therapy (CPT)

Drawing on cognitive theory and learning theory, CPT was developed by psychologist Patricia Resick in 1988. According to CPT, our minds make sense of the world by organizing the information we receive into mental frameworks called *schemas* (patterns of thoughts and behaviors based on memories and experiences that guide our understanding of concepts, our behavior in specific situations, and our view of ourselves and others). Our schemas constantly update as we learn new information and have new experiences. From a CPT perspective, healing from a traumatic event is hindered by the development of stuck points in our schemas—extreme, inaccurate thoughts such as *The world is unsafe.*

CPT helps us get unstuck by examining our negative thoughts and painful emotions. Your therapist will help you identify and resolve these stuck points by leading you through a series of questions designed to challenge their accuracy. By the end of the process, most individuals adjust and update their schemas with more balanced, helpful thoughts (such as *Some things are unsafe, but a lot of people and places are safe*), resulting in a reduction of PTSD symptoms.

Somatic Experiencing (SE)

Created by psychologist Peter Levine in the 1970s, somatic experiencing (SE) is based on the idea that traumatic memories are held in the body as well as the mind, that emotions have a physical effect on the body, and that emotions can resurface suddenly if you encounter a reminder of a trauma. From an SE perspective, symptoms of PTSD are expressions of stress activation and an incomplete defensive reaction to a traumatic event; through increasing tolerance of body sensations and emotions and then inviting a discharge process of the activation, symptoms will dissipate. Therapists must be certified in somatic experiencing to provide this therapy, so be sure to look for this certification if you're interested in pursuing SE.

Internal Family Systems (IFS)

Developed by psychologist Richard Schwartz in the 1980s and similar to ego-state theory mentioned in chapter seven, IFS is a psychotherapy that proposes multiplicity of the personality is a healthy, normative state. IFS takes the stance that everyone has a core self (equivalent to our DBT wise mind) as well as different parts (just like a family consists of different family members) that each have their own perspectives and emotions, and each wants what's best for the self. The goal of IFS is to help people access their core self and heal their wounded parts by changing the dynamics of the self-system (like an internal form of family therapy!).

IFS is a form of talk therapy in which, rather than focusing on memories, you work with your therapist to identify and understand your parts (much like we began to do in chapter seven). Some parts may be more affected by trauma than others; the goal is to understand why some parts are hurting and learn to help them and increase compassion toward them.

The following chart summarizes these therapies to help you decide which therapy might be the best fit for you. Keep in mind that this is only a handful of the many options for trauma processing.

Therapy	Description	Evidence for PTSD	Is homework required?	Requires discussion of trauma?	Can be done virtually?
EMDR	A structured therapy involving brief focus on the trauma memory while experiencing dual attention stimulus (such as eye movements).	Strong evidence for reducing symptoms of PTSD and improving functioning.	No	No	Yes
PE	A cognitive-behavioral therapy involving repeated exposures to the trauma memory and triggers to reduce anxiety through habituation.	Strong evidence for reducing symptoms of PTSD and improving functioning.	Yes	Yes	Yes
CPT	A cognitive-behavioral therapy that involves identifying and challenging maladaptive thoughts and beliefs about the trauma, as well as writing and reading a narrative of the trauma.	Strong evidence for reducing symptoms of PTSD and improving functioning.	Yes	No	Yes
Somatic Experiencing	A therapy that focuses on resolving the physiological and emotional effects of trauma by releasing stored energy in the body through focusing on movement and sensations.	Limited evidence for reducing symptoms of PTSD and improving functioning.	No	No	Yes
IFS	A therapy that views the mind as composed of different parts that have their own perspectives and emotions; helps the client understand their parts and learn to access Self energy to heal parts.	Limited evidence for reducing symptoms of PTSD and improving functioning.	No	No	Yes

Wrapping Up

Recovery from CPTSD is a journey, and it's different for everyone. But no matter how long or intensely you've been struggling, remember that your symptoms started as an adaptive response to help you survive. Your internal system (your ANS, and your parts) has helped you get this far and I have every confidence that you can continue this journey to find the life you deserve—your life worth living.

My goals in this workbook have been to help you understand that your experience makes sense and is understandable, given what you've been through; to ensure you know you're not alone, and that there is hope; and to provide you with the knowledge and tools to help you on this journey. I hope that I've accomplished those goals and I wish you safe travels!

Resources

Further Reading

Boon, S., K. Steele, and O. van der Hart. 2011. *Coping with Trauma-Related Dissociation: Skills Training for Patients and Therapists*. New York: W. W. Norton.

Dana, D. 2021. *Anchored: How to Befriend Your Nervous System Using Polyvagal Theory*. Louisville, CO: Sounds True.

Fisher, J. 2021. *Transforming the Living Legacy of Trauma: A Workbook for Survivors and Therapists*. Eau Claire, WI: PESI.

Kabat-Zinn, J. 1994. *Wherever You Go, There You Are: Mindfulness Meditation in Everyday Life*. New York: Hyperion.

Maté, G. 2004. *When the Body Says No: The Cost of Hidden Stress*. Toronto: Vintage Canada.

Sapolsky, R. M. 1994. *Why Zebras Don't Get Ulcers: A Guide to Stress, Stress Related Diseases, and Coping*. New York: W. H. Freeman.

van der Kolk, B. A. 2014. *The Body Keeps the Score: Brain, Mind, And Body in the Healing of Trauma*. New York: Penguin.

Williams, M., J. Teasdale, Z. Segal, and J. Kabat-Zinn. 2007. *The Mindful Way Through Depression: Freeing Yourself from Chronic Unhappiness*. New York: Guilford Press.

Mindfulness Apps

Insight Timer: https://insighttimer.com

Smiling Mind: https://www.smilingmind.com.au/smiling-mind-app

UCLA Mindful: https://www.uclahealth.org/marc/ucla-mindful-app

Healthy Minds: https://hminnovations.org/meditation-app

Associations

Eye Movement Desensitization and Reprocessing International Association (EMDRIA): https://www.emdria.org/about-emdr-therapy

International Society for the Study of Trauma and Dissociation (ISSTD): https://www.isst-d.org/public-resources-home

References

Beil, K., and D. Hanes. 2013. "The Influence of Urban Natural and Built Environments on Physiological and Psychological Measures of Stress—A Pilot Study." *International Journal of Environmental Research and Public Health* 10(4): 1250–1267.

Bevans, K., A. Cerbone, and S. Overstreet. 2008. "Relations Between Recurrent Trauma Exposure and Recent Life Stress and Salivary Cortisol Among Children." *Development and Psychopathology* 20(1): 257–272. https://doi.org/10.1017/S0954579408000126.

Bonaz, B., V. Sinniger, and S. Pellissier. 2017. "The Vagus Nerve in the Neuro-Immune Axis: Implications in the Pathology of the Gastrointestinal Tract." *Frontiers in Immunology* 8: 1452. https://doi.org/10.3389/fimmu.2017.01452.

Brown, B. 2012. *Daring Greatly: How the Courage to Be Vulnerable Transforms the Way We Live, Love, Parent, and Lead.* New York: Gotham Books.

Cloitre, M., M. Shevlin, C. R. Brewin, J. I. Bisson, N. P. Roberts, A. Maercker, T. Karatzias, and P. Hyland. 2018. "The International Trauma Questionnaire: Development of a Self-Report Measure of *ICD-11* PTSD and Complex PTSD." *Acta Psychiatrica Scandinavica* 138(6): 536–546. https://doi.org/10.1111/acps.12956.

Dana, D. 2018. *The Polyvagal Theory in Therapy: Engaging the Rhythm of Regulation.* New York: W. W. Norton.

———. 2023. "A Beginner's Guide to Polyvagal Theory." *Rhythm of Regulation.* https://www.rhythmofregulation.com/s/Deb-Danas-Beginners-Guide-mk82.pdf.

Emmons, R. A., and M. E. McCullough. 2003. "Counting Blessings Versus Burdens: An Experimental Investigation of Gratitude and Subjective Well-Being in Daily Life." *Journal of Personality and Social Psychology* 84(2): 377–389.

Felitti, V. J., R. F. Anda, D. Nordenberg, D. F. Williamson, A. M. Spitz, V. Edwards, M. P. Koss, and J. S. Marks. 1998. "Relationship of Childhood Abuse and Household Dysfunction to Many of the Leading Causes of Death in Adults: The Adverse Childhood Experiences (ACE) Study." *American Journal of Preventive Medicine* 14(4): 245–258. https://doi.org/10.1016/S0749 -3797(98)00017-8.

Fisher, J. 2017. *Healing the Fragmented Selves of Trauma Survivors: Overcoming Internal Self-Alienation.* New York: Routledge.

———. 2019. "Sensorimotor Psychotherapy in the Treatment of Trauma." *Practice Innovations* 4(3): 156–165.

Fraser, G. A. 1991. "The Dissociative Table Technique: A Strategy for Working with Ego States in Dissociative Disorders and Ego-State Therapy." *Dissociation* 4(4): 205–213.

Gold, S. 2008. "Benefits of a Contextual Approach to Understanding and Treating Complex Trauma." *Journal of Trauma & Dissociation* 9(2): 269–292.

Herman, J. 1992. *Trauma and Recovery: The Aftermath of Violence—From Domestic Abuse to Political Terror.* New York: Basic Books.

Holt-Lunstad, J., T. B. Smith, M. Baker, T. Harris, and D. Stephenson. 2015. "Loneliness and Social Isolation as Risk Factors for Mortality: A Meta-Analytic Review." *Perspectives on Psychological Science* 10(2): 227–237.

International Society for the Study of Trauma and Dissociation Task Force (ISSTDTS). 2023. "EMDR Therapy Basic Training Manual, 2023–2024." Course manual.

Kilpatrick, D. G., H. S. Resnick, M. E. Milanak, M. W. Miller, K. M. Keyes, and M. J. Friedman. 2013. "National Estimates of Exposure to Traumatic Events and PTSD Prevalence Using *DSM-IV* and *DSM-5* Criteria." *Journal of Traumatic Stress* 26(5): 537–547.

Koenen, K., A. Ratanatharathorn, L. Ng, K. McLaughlin, E. Bromet, D. Stein, R. Kessler, et al. 2017. "Posttraumatic Stress Disorder in the World Mental Health Surveys." *Psychological Medicine* 47(13): 2260–2274. https://doi.org/10.1017/S0033291717000708.

Linehan, M. M. 1993. *Cognitive-Behavioral Treatment of Borderline Personality Disorder.* New York: Guilford Press.

————. 2014. *DBT Skills Training Manual*, 2nd ed. New York: Guilford Press.

Meichenbaum, D. 2017. *The Evolution of Cognitive Behavior Therapy: A Personal and Professional Journey with Don Meichenbaum*. New York: Routledge.

Nijenhuis, E. R. S., and E. van der Hart. 2011. "Dissociation in Trauma: A New Definition and Comparison with Previous Formulations." *Journal of Trauma & Dissociation* 12(4): 416–445.

Pachter, L. M., L. Lieberman, S. L. Bloom, and J. A. Fein. 2017. "Developing a Community-Wide Initiative to Address Childhood Adversity and Toxic Stress: A Case Study of the Philadelphia ACE Task Force." *Academic Pediatrics* 17(7S): S130–S135.

Picci, G., N. Christopher-Hayes, N. Petro, B. Taylor, J. Eastman, M. Frenzel, Y. Wang, J. Stephen, V. Calhoun, and T. Wilson. 2022. "Amygdala and Hippocampal Subregions Mediate Outcomes Following Trauma During Typical Development: Evidence from High-Resolution Structural MRI." *Neurobiology of Stress* 18: 100456.

Porges, S. W. 1995. "Orienting in a Defensive World: Mammalian Modifications of Our Evolutionary Heritage. A Polyvagal Theory." *Psychophysiology* 32(4): 301–318.

Schwartz, A. 2016. *The Complex PTSD Workbook: A Mind-Body Approach to Regaining Emotional Control and Becoming Whole*. New York: Althea Press.

Schwartz, R. C. 1995. *Internal Family Systems Therapy*. New York: Guilford Press.

Shapiro, F. 2018. *Eye Movement Desensitization and Reprocessing (EMDR) Therapy: Basic Principles, Protocols, and Procedures*, 3rd ed. New York: Guilford Press.

Sheldon, K. M., and S. Lyubomirsky. 2007. "How to Increase and Sustain Positive Emotion: The Effects of Expressing Gratitude and Visualizing Best Possible Selves." *Journal of Positive Psychology* 1(2): 73–82.

Siegel, D. J. 1999. *The Developing Mind: Toward a Neurobiology of Interpersonal Experience*. New York: Guilford Press.

————. 2014. *Brainstorm: The Power and Purpose of the Teenage Brain*. New York: Jeremy P. Tarcher/Penguin.

Siegel, D. J., and T. P. Bryson. 2011. *The Whole-Brain Child: 12 Revolutionary Strategies to Nurture Your Child's Developing Mind*. London: Bantam Books.

Telles, S., R. S. Mohapatra, and K. V. Naveen. 2005. "Heart Rate Variability Spectrum During Vipassana Mindfulness Meditation." *Journal of Indian Psychology* 23(2): 1–5.

US Department of Veterans Affairs. n.d. "How Common Is PTSD in Adults?" https://www.ptsd .va.gov/understand/common/common_adults.asp.

van der Hart, O., E. R. S. Nijenhuis, and K. Steele. 2006. *The Haunted Self: Structural Dissociation and the Treatment of Chronic Traumatization.* New York: W. W. Norton.

van der Kolk, B. A. 2005. "Developmental Trauma Disorder: Toward a Rational Diagnosis for Children with Complex Trauma Histories." *Psychiatric Annals* 35(5): 401–408. https://doi .org/10.3928/00485713-20050501-06.

———. 2014. *The Body Keeps the Score: Brain, Mind, and Body in the Healing of Trauma.* New York: Viking.

Van Dijk, S. 2013. *DBT Made Simple: A Step-by-Step Guide to Dialectical Behavior Therapy.* Oakland, CA: New Harbinger Publications.

———. 2022. *The DBT Workbook for Emotional Relief: Fast-Acting Dialectical Behavior Therapy Skills to Balance Out-of-Control Emotions and Find Calm Right Now.* Oakland, CA: New Harbinger Publications.

Walker, R. J. 2018. "Polyvagal Theory Chart of Trauma Response." *Southwest Trauma Training.*

Wang, X., and C. Song. 2023. "The Impact of Gratitude Interventions on Patients with Cardiovascular Disease: A Systematic Review." *Frontiers in Psychology* 14: 1243598. https://doi.org/10.3389/fpsyg.2023.1243598.

Watkins, J. G., and H. H. Watkins. 1997. *Ego-States: Theory and Therapy.* New York: W. W. Norton.

Wood, A. M., S. Joseph, J. Lloyd, and S. Atkins. 2009. "Gratitude Influences Sleep Through the Mechanism of Pre-Sleep Cognitions." *Journal of Psychosomatic Research* 66(1): 43–48.

Sheri Van Dijk, MSW, is a psychotherapist and renowned dialectical behavior therapy (DBT) expert. She is author of many books with New Harbinger, including *Don't Let Your Emotions Run Your Life for Teens* and *The DBT Workbook for Emotional Relief.* Her work has focused on using DBT skills to help people manage their emotions and cultivate lasting well-being. In recent years, Sheri has been specializing in complex trauma.

Real change *is* possible

For more than fifty years, New Harbinger has published proven-effective self-help books and pioneering workbooks to help readers of all ages and backgrounds improve mental health and well-being, and achieve lasting personal growth. In addition, our spirituality books offer profound guidance for deepening awareness and cultivating healing, self-discovery, and fulfillment.

Founded by psychologist Matthew McKay and Patrick Fanning, New Harbinger is proud to be an independent, employee-owned company. Our books reflect our core values of integrity, innovation, commitment, sustainability, compassion, and trust. Written by leaders in the field and recommended by therapists worldwide, New Harbinger books are practical, accessible, and provide real tools for real change.

 **newharbinger**publications

MORE BOOKS from
NEW HARBINGER PUBLICATIONS

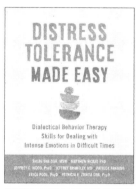

Did you know there are **free tools** you can download for this book?

Free tools are things like **worksheets**, **guided meditation exercises**, and **more** that will help you get the most out of your book.

You can download free tools for this book— whether you bought or borrowed it, in any format, from any source—from the New Harbinger website. All you need is a NewHarbinger.com account. Just use the URL provided in this book to view the free tools that are available for it. Then, click on the "download" button for the free tool you want, and follow the prompts that appear to log in to your NewHarbinger.com account and download the material.

You can also save the free tools for this book to your **Free Tools Library** so you can access them again anytime, just by logging in to your account! Just look for this button on the book's free tools page. ➔ **+ Save this to my free tools library**